The Tragedy
of the
Royal Tar

The 1836 Circus Steamship Fire

MARK WARNER

DownEast Books
Camden, Maine

Published by Down East Books
A wholly owned subsidiary of The Rowman & Littlefield Publishing Group, Inc.
4501 Forbes Boulevard, Suite 200, Lanham, Maryland 20706
www.rowman.com

Unit A, Whitacre Mews, 26-34 Stannary Street, London SE11 4AB

Distributed by NATIONAL BOOK NETWORK

Library of Congress Cataloging-in-Publication Data Available

ISBN 978-1-60893-357-0 (pbk. : alk. paper)
ISBN 978-1-60893-358-7 (electronic)

♾™ The paper used in this publication meets the minimum requirements of
American National Standard for Information Sciences—Permanence of Paper for
Printed Library Materials, ANSI/NISO Z39.48-1992.

Printed in the United States of America

To Helen
For too many reasons

Acknowledgments

I would like to express my sincere thanks to the following organizations and individuals who helped me with information about the Royal Tar and/or helped with photos and art work. They are in no particular order. My apologies for any omissions.

Queens County Historical Society, Gagetown, New Brunswick; Provincial Archives, Fredericton, New Brunswick; Tim Ronk, Houston Public Library, Houston Library; Portland, Maine Historical Society, Portland, Maine; Lighthouse Museum, Rockland, Maine; Mystic Seaport, Mystic, Connecticut; Museum of Maritime History, Halifax, Nova Scotia; Bill Chilles and the gang at the Vinalhaven Historical Society, Vinalhaven, Maine; Jamie Serran, Yarmouth County Museum & Archives, Yarmouth, Nova Scotia; Lois Lutton (Olive family descendent) Saint John, New Brunswick; Nathan Lipfert and Kelly Page, Maine Maritime Museum, Bath, Maine; Castine Historical Society, Castine, Maine; United States Coast Guard; Gary Hughes, Christine Little, and Janet Bishop, New Brunswick Museum Archives & Research Library, Saint John, New Brunswick; Martin Lanthier, Library and Archives Canada, Ottawa, Ontario; New Brunswick Firefighters Museum, Saint John, New Brunswick; Julie Sopher, Shelburne Museum, Shelburne, Vermont; Ben Fuller, Penobscot Marine Museum, Searsport, Maine; Nancy Meagher, Bank of America; Judith Griffin, Circus Historical Society; Terry Ariano, Somers Historical Society, Somers, New York; Heidi Taylor and Jennifer Lemmer Posey at the Ringling Museum of Art, Sarasota, Florida; The Ward Chapman Library, University of New Brunswick, Saint John, New Brunswick; Saint John Public Library, Saint John, New Brunswick; Saint John Historical Society, Saint John, New

Brunswick; Fred Dahlinger, Circus Historical Society; Lucy Kuemmerle for the manuscript read and suggestions. Special thanks to Steve Busch for his rendition of the *Royal Tar* disaster, and, last, but not least, Michael Steere for the great design work and editing.

Contents

Prologue

On a brisk fall day in October of 1836, a steam-powered sailing vessel caught fire in Penobscot Bay, Maine. On board, in addition to its regular passengers, was a small circus menagerie of assorted animals, including an elephant. The fire quickly spread and consumed the vessel. Thirty-two people and all of the animals died. On the nearby island of Vinalhaven, workers were finishing the chimney on a house they had just completed. Spotting the fire, they sat on the ridgepole and had front row seats to witness the tragedy unfolding a little over a mile away.

I grew up in that house on Vinalhaven and heard many tales surrounding the *Royal Tar* and the fate of her animals. On rainy

The author sits on the same roof witnesses sat on in 1836 to watch the *Royal Tar* tragedy unfold out in Penobscot Bay. (Jennifer Warner)

days, my parents would entice me out from underfoot and suggest searching the shore for tiger teeth, elephant bones or other artifacts from the steamer. Despite long hours climbing over wet, seaweed covered rocks along the shore, I never found a thing, but my interest in that long ago event persisted. Herein is the story of the *Royal Tar*, as complete as I could make it using what information still exists.

Any errors or mistakes are entirely mine.

The Beginning

It is a hot, steamy, summer morning in 1835. A three-masted bark, the Governor English, *slowly emerges from the fog outside the harbor at Saint John, New Brunswick, Canada. She has been waiting for slack tide and the ever present morning fog to lift. What little wind there is finally enables the ship to creep into the harbor. Slowly making her way to the Saint John waterfront, her captain finds space at the end of South Market Wharf. After the square rigger is tied up, her passengers, mostly immigrants from Europe, slowly disembark. Their legs are wobbly after weeks at sea and they find it difficult to stand on the solid wharf. Two of those trying to get their land legs back are John Braxton, a recent widower from Ireland, and his ten year old son William. They are headed for a new life in America via New Brunswick as the* Governor English *was the only ship they could get space on. They plan on staying the winter in Saint John, saving enough money to book passage to America next year.*

Every tale has a beginning and the story of the *Royal Tar* starts at the end of Market Street in Carleton, New Brunswick, Canada, in 1835. Today, the area is called the West End and lies across the Saint John River from the city of Saint John. When the *Royal Tar* was built, New Brunswick was a major exporter of ship building wood, mostly to Great Britain, America, and the West Indies. While Great Britain and America had access to various hardwoods, Canada had mostly soft woods such as black and white spruce, yellow birch, white pine and larch (tamarac, hackmatack, cypress, or juniper). The use of these woods caused Canadian ships of that period to be called "soft-wood vessels." To satisfy demand, a number of shipyards in and around Saint John turned out a large number of ships to carry lumber to the buyers. One of the more prolific shipyards belonged to the Olive family, who eventually built a total of

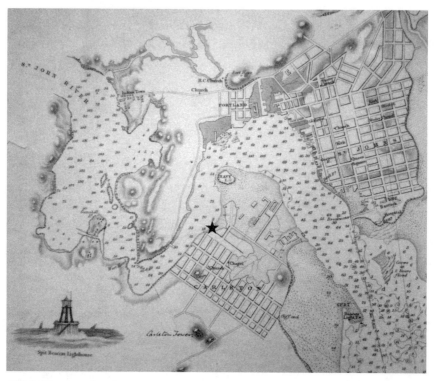

1832 harbor map showing Carlton and Saint John. The star marks the location of the Olive Shipyard that built the *Royal Tar*. (New Brunswick Museum, Saint John, New Brunswick M243-1832q)

The Tragedy of the *Royal Tar*

ninety-five vessels, including ten paddle wheel steamboats, one of which was the *Royal Tar.*

Born in 1755, William Olive had learned his trade in Great Britain and, at an unknown date, made his way to America where he joined other immigrants who, like himself, remained loyal to their home country. William was thirty at the close of the Revolutionary War, when he and his wife, along with other Loyalists, boarded a ship for Saint John. Arriving in late July, William discovered that most of the lands in Saint John, on the east side of the river, had already been taken. He managed to obtain land on the west side, then called Carleton, and eventually established a shipyard along the Saint John River at the north end of Market Street. By 1816, aided by his two sons, William Junior and Isaac, he had turned out six vessels. William Senior died in 1822 at the age of sixty-nine and his two sons took over the operation of the shipyard.

By 1835, William Junior and Isaac had constructed nineteen sailing vessels and one paddle wheel steamer, the *John Ward.* This vessel was one of the first steamboats to operate between Saint John and Fredericton (later the capital of New Brunswick), running up and down the Saint John River. Also, in 1835, they began work on another paddle wheel steamer, the *Royal Tar.*

In those days a vessel did not usually spring from an architect's plan but began as a wooden half model. It was literally, only a half, as if the carver had made a complete model and then split it down the middle. It was a scaled down version of the vessel to be built. The block that the builder carved from was usually made up of several horizontal pieces called "lifts," held together by two or three wooden pegs. After carving, the half model was disassembled by removing the pegs and each "lift" was accurately measured. These measurements were then transferred to the painted white floor of the lofting shed but enlarged according to the scale of the model (normally one quarter or one half inch to the foot). The goal of this procedure was to reproduce full size drawings of the frames (or ribs), stem, and stern post on the loft's floor. These were then used to make thin wooden patterns which would transfer the original half model's lines from the floor to the major structural members that would form the basic skeleton of the vessel.

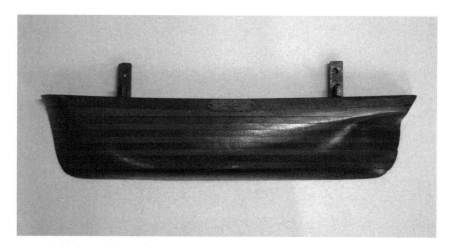

Early nineteenth-century ships started out as a half model. Horizontal sections, called lifts, were disassembled and carefully measured. (Model courtesy of the Maine Maritime Museum, Bath, Maine)

These large hull timbers were too big to be steam bent to shape and were sawn out of straight pieces, either cut at the yard itself or obtained from a local sawmill. There, the lumber would have been sawn to the yard's specifications and hauled to the Market Street shipyard.

The thin patterns from the loft were placed on top of the timbers and their shapes traced with chalk, a pencil, or a nail. The wood, usually white spruce or larch, was then cut by hand at a saw-

The Tragedy of the *Royal Tar*

ing pit. This was either an actual pit dug in the ground about six feet deep or a platform built about six feet above the level. The sawing was done by two men, the more experienced on top. He guided the blade along the scribed marks and the bottom man did the bulk of the work by pulling down on the saw.

When it was time to begin construction, three-foot-long blocks of wood, called keel blocks, were laid out in a straight line perpendicular to the un-built keel. Two more blocks were then placed on top of every two keel blocks, at right angles. A final block was added on top. It would be at right angles to the keel. This "crib" of blocks was about three feet square and three feet high and would allow room for the men to work under the hull. The keel itself, usually of yellow birch sections bolted together, was then placed on the keel block cribs. Next, the stern post and stem were erected and bolted to the keel. The exact locations for the frames were scribed on top of the keel.

Because the saws of the time couldn't make the curves necessary for the fames, they were made up in sections, laid out on a framing platform. This was placed next to or right over the keel. A straight piece of timber would form the ship's floor. Shorter pieces, called futtocks, were bolted on the floor ends to form a crude curve. The upper-most top pieces came next; all forming a single frame. As each was made up, they were stacked on the framing platform, ready for assembly.

The crew then carried each assembled frame to its position on the keel. Using poles and tackles, each frame was raised to the vertical and temporarily held in position until bolted to the keel. The frames for vessels then were quite large. Those for the *Royal Tar* were massive, perhaps six to eight inches square and the spacing between frames was only a few inches. Once all the frames were in place, the keelson was placed on top of the floors and ran the length of the vessel. Like the keel, the keelson was usually made up

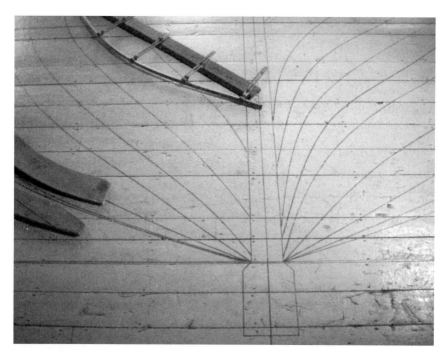

Measurements from a half
model were scaled up on the
floor of the lofting shed. From
these, full scale patterns, or
moulds, were made to transfer
the lines to the framing platform. (Lofting shed floor courtesy of the Maine Maritime
Museum, Bath, Maine)

of two or three sections bolted down
through the floors into the keel below.
Keelsons might consist of two or three
layers stacked one on top of another.
They added strength to the hull and
helped tie the floors together.
Everything was then checked for
straightness, and planking of the inside
of the hull could begin.

This inside planking, called the ceiling, added additional
strength to the hull and protected the frames from shifting cargo.
Thicker than the outside planking, the ceiling could have been
made up of planks as thick as five inches. These planks were fastened to the inside of the frames with iron bolts or, more likely,

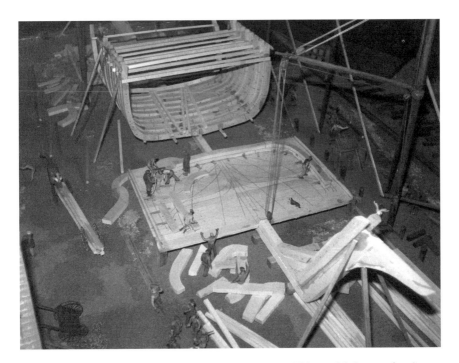

This model shows a framing platform over the keel. Sections of each frame were assembled here, using the lines from the lofting floor transferred by the moulds. Frames were made in pairs and bolted together so no butt joints overlapped. The completed frames were hoisted into position and bolted to the keel. (Bank of America)

wooden dowels called trunnels. They were driven into holes bored through the ceiling planks and into the frames. Before being driven, the ends were split with a small saw. Small wooden wedges were then driven into the splits to lock the trunnels in place. The ends of the trunnels were then cut flush. When launched, the wood, including the trunnels, would swell, locking everything together.

Once the ceiling was in place, the outside planking would begin. Again, the planks were attached to the frames by trunnels with some bolts added in strategic places. Heavy knees were now installed to help support the deck. These were cut from the crooks of tree branches, or sometimes roots, and looked like large wooden right angles. Longitudinal timbers were placed on top of the knees to provide a shelf for the deck beam ends to rest on.

To make the steamer watertight, oakum (twisted jute or hemp) was pounded into the seams between the outside planks. Oakum was obtained by picking apart and unraveling the fibers from old sailing ships' rigging. The resulting furry mass was then loosely twisted into soft "rope." Oakum shops also spun the stuff from raw hemp. Thomas Jefferson, commenting on proper attire for American Supreme Court Justices, said, "Discard the monstrous wig which makes English Judges look like rats peeping through bunches of oakum." Jefferson drafted the Declaration of Independence on paper made from hemp, which contains 250% more fiber than cotton. Currently, hemp is grown throughout the world, except the

A replica frame, or rib, of a vessel approximately the size of the *Royal Tar*. It clearly shows the outer planking and thicker inner ceiling. (New Brunswick Museum, Saint John, New Brunswick)

United States. Canada, Great Britain, China, France, Russia, and Spain are the chief producers. Farming hemp is banned in America because it is genetically related to marijuana.

Once the oakum was pounded between the hull planks, hot tar was slopped into the cracks to seal them. It was hot and messy labor, and men frequently got as much tar on themselves as into the cracks. It was not unusual for workers to suffer deep burns.

All the work of building a vessel like the *Royal Tar* was essentially done by hand. To build a steamer of her size would have entailed a yard crew on the order of thirty or forty men. Some were highly skilled, while others were merely laborers. A good planking crew could put three to five strakes (planks) on a hull in a day, typically ten hours long.

Before the decks were installed, the *Royal Tar's* boilers and major engine parts, such as the cylinder and piston, would have been hauled up and carefully lowered into the hull, then fastened to floor timbers and any special frames. Then the decks would have been installed, caulked with oakum, and sealed with tar. The massive paddle wheels and their protective paddle boxes were then installed, as well as the rudder. Deck houses and the pilot house were added and everything was given a coat of paint.

The *Royal Tar* was built as a steam powered two-masted schooner. Each of her masts was in two sections. The bottom sections would have been hoisted up with poles and tackles, lowered into the hull, and their butt ends stepped into notches cut into the keelson. They were then supported with standing rigging fastened to chain plates on the sides of the hull. The upper sections, called topmasts, were then raised and set in place at the tops of the lower masts. These also were supported by standing rigging, usually of tarred hemp. Because of the thirty-foot tides in Saint John, it might have been more practical to put the masts in after launching. The *Royal Tar* would have been secured alongside a wharf and, at low tide, the masts lowered down into her, but there is no record to indicate that this was done.

When the *Royal Tar* was ready to be launched into the river, she was essentially complete and resting on her keel blocks. Long timbers, called ground ways, were laid parallel to the keel. These were heavily greased, usually with tallow. A second set of timbers, called sliding ways, were then placed on top of the greased ground ways. Using large sledges, wedges were driven between the keel and the keel blocks until the hull was slightly raised above the keel blocks, perhaps only a half inch. Additional timbers, at right angles to the hull, were then slid under the keel and became the foundation for a huge cradle. After it was bolted together, the keel block wedges were removed and the hull settled onto the cradle. The steamer was then ready to be launched. She slid into the river at high tide on Monday, November 5, 1835, to the traditional cries of, "There she goes." Launchings were great forms of entertainment in those days, and no doubt a large crowd was on hand for the occasion. The crews' wives and girlfriends, kids, dogs, and maybe even a band livened up the affair. Once afloat, the vessel was towed to a nearby wharf for her final fitting out.

Very little remains today of the area where the *Royal Tar* was built. The Olive shipyard at the end of Market Street closed toward the end of the nineteenth century. A lumber yard eventually occupied the same area until the mid-nineteen hundreds when construction began for a new bridge across the harbor. This was coupled to Route 1 along the Saint John River. The new on-off ramp for the West End (what used to be called Carleton) was built pretty much on where the Olive shipyard used to be. Unfortunately, the birthplace of the *Royal Tar* is now mostly buried in concrete and steel and, like the steamer herself, lost forever.

The location of the Olive Shipyard is now buried under a highway on-ramp at the end of Market Place on the West End, formerly Carleton. (Helen Warner)

Saint John

John Braxton has found lodgings for himself and William in a boarding house off King Street, at the top of the hill in Saint John. It is a single room with two beds and the rent includes meals. William will start school in three days and so is able to take it easy for a while. John is a blacksmith by trade and has found a job in a local blacksmith shop on Water Street. Will (as he prefers to be called) spends his time exploring the city, especially along the wharves. For a ten-year-old boy, it is an exciting place, crowded with sailing ships, all tied up alongside each other with the inner ones fastened securely to wharves. At low tide, and Will has never seen such a low tide, the ships all sit on their keels. Men move cargo to and from the vessels on low-slung horse-drawn wagons called slovens. They go right out onto the muddy and gravel bottom to get as close to the ships as possible. When not poking around the waterfront, and getting underfoot, Will likes to visit his father in the blacksmith shop. It is warm there, even hot, with forges roaring and hammers clanging, all in the business of creating special hardware for Saint John's bustling shipyards.

arleton, where the *Royal Tar* was built, lies across the Saint John River from the city of Saint John, then, as now, the largest city in the Canadian Province of New Brunswick. Located on the northwest side of the Bay of Fundy, Saint John is about one third of the way between the Maine border and Amherst, Nova Scotia, at the head of the bay. The closest Maine town is Calais, and it is about sixty miles from Saint John. Driving by automobile on Route 1, the trip takes about an hour and a half. On a good day and weather permitting, the *Royal Tar* would have made the fifty miles to Eastport, the nearest town to Calais, in approximately five hours.

Saint John is a hilly city and many of its buildings are made of brick. They were originally wood until a devastating fire in 1877 destroyed most of them. Apparently a spark, from an unknown source, ignited some hay near the waterfront in the area called Market Square. It had been a dry and warm June and that Wednesday was windy. Within a short time, a majority of Saint John's business district was on fire. When it was all over, some sixteen hundred business buildings and homes had been destroyed.

Currier & Ives print of the 1877 Saint John fire that destroyed much of the city. (Saint John Firefighters, Museum)

Nineteen or twenty people died and many more were injured. Although many folks left Saint John, others remained and rebuilt the city, with help from around the world. Even today, that June day in 1877 is referred to as Black Wednesday.

At the time of the fire, the city's streets were merely packed dirt. There were probably wooden sidewalks here and there so people could get out of the dust and mud. There may have been some cobblestones on a few waterfront streets when ballast stones were dumped ashore. Most of the commerce was centered near the river and the shore was lined with wharves. The tide in this area ranges about thirty feet between high and low. Ships were brought into the wharves at high tide and secured. When the tide went out,

This late 1800s photograph of Market Slip illustrates the Saint John waterfront at low tide. Little would have changed since the time of the *Royal Tar*. Special low-slung wagons, called slovens, were used to transfer cargo between ship and shore. (Provincial Archives New Brunswick Isaac Erb Photo: P11-20)

ships were stranded on the muddy bottom. While this made it difficult to unload or load cargo, it gave easy access to ships bottoms for any repairs or painting.

Saint John's harbor is ice free, making it an important international port. Forestry products, so important in the *Royal Tar*'s day, continue to be a vital export. Half the world's supply of potash (used in commercial fertilizers) is found in New Brunswick and is exported through the port. Canada's first public museum (1842) is now the new and excellent New Brunswick Museum, located in Market Square. The world's first steam powered foghorn was invented in Saint John, where the harbor is notorious for its summer fog. A less well known invention (and perhaps less welcome) to come from the city was the first clockwork driven time bomb in 1880. Notable citizens from Saint John include actors Walter Pigeon and Donald Southerland (perhaps most famous for his role as a surgeon in the movie *M*A*S*H*). A less notable temporary resident was the American traitor Benedict Arnold, who lived in the city from 1786-1791, arriving three years after William Olive settled in Carleton.

Various European explorers visited the mouth of the Saint John River in the early 1500s but it was the French explorer Samuel de Champlain who gave the area its name. He arrived on June 24, 1604, which was Saint Jean de Baptist Day and named the river in the saint's honor. Occupied at different times by the British and the French, Saint John was inundated by British Loyalists displaced from America in the 1780s. Because of their loyalty to the Crown, these folks were offered land to settle on. Thus William Olive arrived in 1783 and was granted a parcel of land in Carleton. In 1785, Saint John became Canada's first incorporated city.

At the time, New Brunswick was heavily forested, and ship building and lumber were major factors in the development of Carleton and Saint John.

View of Saint John and its harbor from the southern end of Carleton. 1848 Lithograph from the John Clarence Webster Canadian Collection. (New Brunswick Museum, Saint John, New Brunswick W1518)

By the time of the *Royal Tar*'s construction, the city had become the largest ship building community in Canada, with a reputation for building ships known for their craftsmanship, speed, and solid construction. Sixteen years after the *Royal Tar* was built, the three-masted clipper ship *Marco Polo* was launched in 1851. Billed as the fastest ship in the world, she set many speed records, both as a passenger vessel and cargo ship. She sprang a bad leak in 1883 and was beached at Prince Edward Island to prevent her sinking. The crew cut her masts down to keep the wind from blowing her farther on shore. Before any repair work could begin, a storm, only a few weeks later, broke her apart, ending her career.

Seeking work and a better life, many immigrants arrived almost daily from Europe, mostly from Scotland and Ireland. The 1834 census showed a population of 12,000. Life was not easy then and those financially able headed south for greener pastures in America. This created the need for a suitable vessel to transport them. Three local businessmen contracted for the construction of a steam powered vessel that would make weekly runs between Saint John and Portland, Maine. The job of building such a boat went to the William and Isaac Olive shipyard across the river in Carleton. It would be named the *Royal Tar*, in honor of King William. Apparently he was quite a sailor and since sailors were called tars, it seemed appropriate to name the vessel after the King.

Launchings themselves were a popular spectator sport and many people would have lined the river banks to watch the event. Not all launchings went according to plan. The *Belvidere,* a six-hundred-ton ship built by the Olive brothers and launched in 1835 provided much more of an event than anyone could have predicted. She was launched fully rigged, with all her masts and topmasts in place. Her deck was crowded with guests and a band no doubt played some lively tunes to suit the occasion. The ship slid majestically down the ways into the river and promptly capsized, dumping all of her surprised guests overboard. A newspaper of the time reported that "the voluminous skirts of the ladies buoyed them up until they could be rescued." The *Belvidere* continued to provide amusement as she floated upriver to the reversing falls, got stuck there, and then floated back down when the tide changed. She ended up stranded on a riverside beach where she was finally hauled off and righted. She was then sold and reportedly caught fire in an eastern port. She was eventually lost at sea.

The reversing falls lie a short distance upriver from Carleton, at the first bend in the Saint John River. Technically, these are not falls but rather a set of reversing rapids. The incoming thirty foot tide is stronger than the river current, and creates a series of large eddies, whirlpools, and standing waves heading upriver. The outgoing-tide, now flowing with the current, also creates eddies and waves. In addition, water coursing over ledges causes actual falls in the other direction. Slack periods, between each tide cycle, allow vessels safe transit through the area. This occurs when the tide level equals the natural river level. Slack tide lasts only about twenty minutes, so vessels transiting the area need to make sure they do so at slack tide, otherwise it could be a wild ride. Other reversing falls occur elsewhere in the world, but these may be the largest and certainly the most dramatic.

The reversing falls presented a serious hazard to navigation up and down the Saint John River.

Vessels had to wait until slack tide in order to safely navigate past the falls. There were two slack tides, one past low tide and one past high tide.

Early Indians of the region called the river "Wollaston," which meant "The Beautiful River." It was widely used as transportation for hunting and trade.

Travel between Saint John and Carleton was seriously hindered by the Saint John River. The first bridge to span the river wasn't built until the mid 1800s, so ferries served to get people across. There were at least two operating when the *Royal Tar* was being constructed. The Short ferry ran between the north side of Carleton to the end of Short Ferry Road, directly across the river. It would have landed passengers and freight at the north end of Market Street. A longer ferry operated across the harbor from the foot of

Rodney Street in Carleton to the Saint John waterfront in the vicinity of Princess and Water Streets.

One of the first steamboats to run the river between Saint John and Fredericton, up the Saint John River, was the *John Ward*, also built by the Olive brothers in 1831. Her schedules had to be adjusted each trip in order to navigate the falls at the right time to avoid the rushing currents, and to avoid striking ledges at low tide.

After the *Royal Tar* was launched, without mishap, she was towed to a nearby wharf where she was finished, or fitted out. Final hook-ups of her steam engine were made, her masts put in place and rigged, sails set and checked for proper fit. Bunks and furniture were added to her cabins, wood for her boilers was stowed on board and all the other sundry tasks necessary to get her ready for sea trials were carried out. Her scheduled trips to Portland were to begin in the spring of 1836.

The *Royal Tar*

One Sunday afternoon, three weeks after Will has started school, he and his father walk along the waterfront. They have been talking about the Royal Tar, a new vessel being built across the harbor at Carleton. Will bends over, picks up a flat stone and sends it skipping over the nearby water.

"How did she get that name?" he asks, reaching for another stone and makes the throw. His father watches it make a few hops and sink. "She's named after King William of England," he says. "How does that become Royal Tar?" *asks Will. John thinks for a minute and says, "I guess it's because the King is part of the royal family and likes to sail boats. Sailors are called tars. Put the two together and you get* Royal Tar. *Understand?" "I think so," answers Will. "Did I get my name from the King too?*

It is difficult to know exactly what the *Royal Tar* looked like. There are no photographs and very few pieces of art work available; those that do exist all deal almost exclusively with her on fire. All one can do is draw some conclusions based on features that seem to be consistent from one painting to another. Examining the renderings of other vessels for the same period can also provide clues.

The Saint John Port Registry #23, dated May 3, gives a brief description of the *Royal Tar*. She had two masts, was one hundred and fifty-six feet in length on deck, with a twenty-four foot beam,

Copy of the original Saint John Registrar of Shipping, dated 3 May 1836 for the Royal Tar. It shows her details and registered owners. (Library and Archives Canada/Department of Transport fonds/RG42, Volume 1335)

and she drew twelve feet. She was listed as both a schooner and a steam vessel. Net tonnage was two hundred and fifty. She is listed as having a bowsprit although some paintings of her do not show one. She also is listed as having a square fore-top-sail, although this is often not depicted by artists.

Technically, the *Royal Tar* was a two-masted fore-topsail schooner. The foremast had a gaff rigged foresail with a square top-sail above. Her mainsail (the aftermost sail) was also gaff rigged. Her long bowsprit would have carried at least two jibs. She had passenger cabins, probably most on her main deck with others below. She had a small pilot house mounted above the upper deck cabins and placed forward for visibility. The cabins were for more affluent passengers who desired some level of comfort and privacy. She most likely had an open deck aft, as several accounts of the time mention that she had a canvas awning rigged over the stern area.

Although she had sails, her main propulsion was side mounted paddle wheels, one on each side amidships. Each wheel was about thirty feet in diameter and was enclosed in a paddle box to protect the paddles from floating debris as well as to keep passengers away. Mounted between the paddle boxes, and on top of the cabins, was a huge, very distinctive "A" frame that supported a large

Pilot houses on early nineteenth century steamboats were very simple, basically containing a steering wheel, compass and a means of communicating with the engineer. (Shelburne Museum, Shelburne, Vermont)

horizontal beam. A heavy connecting rod descended downward from each end of the beam. One was connected to the engine below deck while the other connected to a crankshaft that turned the paddle wheels. Immediately forward of the beam were two tall side-by-side smokestacks.

The area below the main deck, in addition to cabins, would have been partially open for cargo storage, most likely forward and aft of the engine room. Crew quarters would have been here, as well as space and accommodations for steerage passengers, possibly some sort of bunk room. If not the latter, steerage passengers had to

Walking beams were massive structures connecting the steam engine below with the paddle wheels at the sides of the vessel. (Shelburne Museum, Shelburne, Vermont)

The Tragedy of the *Royal Tar*

shift for themselves in chairs or lying on deck. The trip to Portland was, after all, only an overnight trip.

There were no regulations at the time concerning the number of passengers a vessel could carry. One account mentions two hundred on board the *Royal Tar* for her maiden voyage around the Saint John harbor. For her final trip to Portland, there were ninety-two or ninety-three listed (one account even had ninety-six). Her crew was normally about twenty-one and included the Captain (Thomas Reed), a mate, the pilot, an engineer and second engineer, four firemen (to keep the boiler fires going), five seamen, two cooks, a steward, a stewardess, and three cabin boys (also doubling as waiters).

Why was the *Royal Tar* both a steamer and sailing vessel? At the time, pure sailing ships were still being built (and continued to be until the end of the century) and the sea-going community was reluctant to embrace the new age of steam. Another reason to keep sails on a steamer was that the engines were not entirely reliable and if one broke down, or they ran out of fuel, they could raise sails and continue on. Sail still ruled for ocean crossings, however, as early steam powered vessels just couldn't carry enough wood to get them to their destinations. Coal, which took up much less space, really didn't come into use until the mid 1800s.

While sail was preferred for ocean passages, the paddle wheel steamer was primarily used for coastal and river travel. Unless there was a problem, steam engines were more dependable than relying on the variability of wind for power. Originally derived from water wheel technology, the paddle wheel offered advantages over a conventional propeller. The latter was still fairly crude, inefficient, and unbalanced. The propeller's vibrations caused leaks in the propeller shaft area. Protruding aft of the keel, propellers were prone to damage when a vessel encountered rocks, ledges, or debris in the water. Vessels with damaged propellers had to be hauled out for repair and

Paddle wheels, such as this one on the steamboat *Ticonderoga,* did not extend very far below the waterline, an advantage in avoiding collisions with ledges below. (Shelburne Museum, Shelburne, Vermont)

there were not that many facilities that could handle boats of that size.

At the time, paddle wheels were more efficient than propellers. In addition, the shafts driving them did not extend through the hull below the waterline; so there were no problems with leaks. The paddles of the *Royal Tar* would have only extended about five or six feet into the water and thus escaped being damaged by rocks and ledges. If a paddle was ever damaged, a crew member or two merely had to enter the paddle box through a small access door and repair, or replace, a paddle with a spare. Early paddle wheels, like those of the *Royal Tar*, had fixed paddles, while later designs had paddles that pivoted and shed water sooner and were more efficient. Paddle wheel steamers, often called paddlers, were in vogue up to the end of the century, when screw type propellers became more efficient and, combined with more powerful engines, could drive a vessel faster and more economically than the paddle wheel.

The *Royal Tar*'s construction was commissioned by three Saint John businessmen. John Hammond had forty shares, John McLaughlin had eight shares and Hugh McKay had sixteen shares. There is no mention anywhere who owned the remainder of the shares but it was not uncommon for the builder to have them. Their shipyard of choice was the Olive yard in Carleton. William and Isaac were helped by their younger brother James, who retired to farming in late 1836.

These old timbers were used to support completed vessels as they slide into the Saint John River. They are in the right location and may be part of the Olive Shipyard that built the *Royal Tar*.

Advertisement from the *New Brunswick Courier*, 1836, notifying immigrants of a means to get to America, the fares, and sailing times. (Courtesy of Saint John Public Library, Saint John, New Brunswick)

During this period, many immigrants came to Saint John in returning lumber ships and many of them were looking for a way to get to America. One way was by stagecoach, which was a long, bumpy, dirty trip over poor roads that might take a week or more. A steamer could make the same trip in a day and a half and for a lesser fare. Hammond, McLaughlin, and McKay saw this as an opportunity to establish regular runs between Saint John and Portland, Maine. From there, passengers could take other steamers to Boston or New York. By an agreement with the Cumberland Steam Navigation Company in Portland, the *Royal Tar* was advertised jointly with those other boats as the "Eastern Steamboat Mail Line." Construction began in 1835 and was finished in the spring of 1836.

The *Royal Tar* as depicted by a local
artist on the anniversary of the
steamboat's tragic end in Penobscot
Bay. (Vinalhaven Historical Society,
Vinalhaven, Maine)

To Portland

It is the first Sunday in May, 1836. The completed Royal Tar *has been moved from Carleton to a wharf on Saint John's waterfront. The first sea trial will be on Monday. Will and a couple of school friends are relaxing in the sun on the end of the wharf, their feet dangling over the edge. It is high tide and Will has a fishing line tied around a piling, but hasn't had a nibble. The boys intensely watch the activity on the* Royal Tar. *There is a line of workers putting boxes on board. Some crew members are aloft, carefully fitting new sails to her spars. Others are putting a coat of paint on the tiny pilot house. The boys are considering skipping school the next day to see the* Royal Tar's *maiden voyage, but know they will get in trouble if they do. They are debating if it would be worth it when Will's fishing line suddenly becomes active. All thoughts of skipping school are forgotten as the boys pull in a good sized pollock.*

After completing her fitting out at Carleton, the *Royal Tar* was moved to the Saint John waterfront for test runs before beginning her regular trips to Portland. The first trial took place on Monday, the second of May, 1836, and it was a grand affair. About two hundred guests were on board as the *Royal Tar* steamed proudly around the harbor. A hot lunch was served and a local newspaper reported that it was accompanied with "rivers of sherry and oceans of champagne."

After several more trials were conducted, the first run to

Market Slip, Saint John, at high tide, in a late 1800's photograph. There would have been little change from earlier times along the waterfront. The *Royal Tar*, because of her size, would have tied up at the end of one of the wharves. (New Brunswick Museum, Saint John, New Brunswick 1989.20)

Portland was made during the second week of May, and then she made weekly trips throughout the summer and fall, with a scheduled stop at Eastport, Maine. There is some evidence that she also made separate runs to Eastport, leaving Saint John at 10:00 on Monday mornings and returning Tuesday. The fare was one dollar per person or two dollars for a cabin.

The trips to Portland left on Wednesdays at seven in the morning, making a stop at Eastport. Passengers and freight would have been unloaded and new passengers and freight put on board. The *Royal Tar* most likely left Eastport early in the evening for the overnight voyage to Portland. Fares from Saint John to Portland were three dollars for deck (steerage) passengers or eight dollars for

The Tragedy of the *Royal Tar*

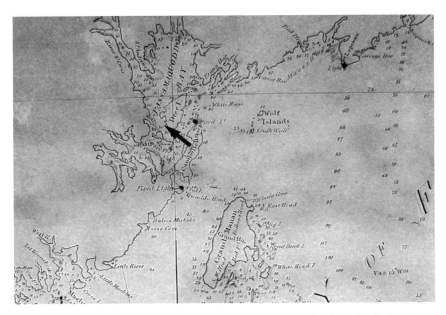

a cabin. It cost an extra five dollars if one wanted to continue to Boston on another steamer.

There is little evidence showing the exact route that the *Royal Tar* would have taken between Saint John and Portland. Navigation was not the sophisticated science it is today. Captain Reed relied on the few crude charts available, a compass and visual references to known landmarks, and he carried a knowledgeable pilot on board for all of his trips. The pilot knew the harbors, rock and ledge locations, shallow spots, and other hazards. He also knew the tides and currents that would affect the voyage. Since much of the trip was at night, the captain and pilot depended on the few lighthouses then located along the coast. There are a little over sixty lighthouses along the Maine coast today but less than half were available for the *Royal Tar*'s trips between

Saint John and Portland. New Brunswick had only four lighthouses that would have been along the steamer's route. They were all lit with whale oil lamps and were little more than lighted beacons, difficult to see from a great distance. Fog, rain, or mist easily obliterated these early lights and vessels would then have to rely on dead reckoning navigation, or simply anchor until conditions improved.

Here is a description of a typical trip to Eastport and on to Portland. She left Saint John in the morning, either from Hanford's Wharf, or North Market Wharf, both at the foot of Duke Street, at seven on a Wednesday. After passing Partridge Island at the mouth of the harbor, she turned southwest for Eastport. This part of the trip was fairly easy, as the New Brunswick coast here has few islands or ledges to pose any threats. The first tangible landmark was the light at Point Lepreau, roughly half way to Passamaquoddy Bay and Eastport. Established in 1831, this lighthouse is now surrounded by grounds of the Point Lepreau Nuclear Generating Plant.

Approaching Passamaquoddy Bay, she would have passed between Campobello Island (Roosevelt's summer home was later located there) and the Canadian mainland. The channel here, straight and deep, follows along the west side of the island for half of its length, about five nautical miles (a nautical mile is 6,000 feet as opposed to the statute mile of 5,280 feet). The town of Eastport lies to the east of Moose Island, and the *Royal Tar* tied up there to discharge passengers and freight. Portland passengers could go ashore while wood was added or stay aboard while in port. She left Eastport for Portland late in the afternoon or early in the evening.

There is a very narrow and shallow channel between Eastport and Campobello Island and the shortest way south, but is unlikely that Captain Reed would have taken it unless he could have left Eastport in daylight hours. In addition, the tide and currents here are formidable. The only time the *Royal Tar* could have safely navigated the channel, called Lubec Narrows, would have been at slack tide. It is more probable that he reversed his course to the northeast, again past the west side of Campobello. It was only a five mile trip and there was a light, Head Harbor (or East Quoddy) Light, on the north end of the island to guide them in the dark. Once around Campobello, Captain Reed could then turn south down the east side of the island in clear waters. By now the evening meal would have been served to the cabin passengers. Steerage people fended for themselves with perhaps sandwiches or wine and bread. The lamps and candles were lit and passengers started to settle down for the overnight trip. The *Royal Tar* was headed for the next lighthouse on the voyage, at West Quoddy Head, only a nautical mile and a half from the southern tip of Campobello.

The light at West Quoddy was built of beach stone in 1808 and is located on the easternmost point of land in the mainland United States. Today, its familiar red and white striped tower is a popular tourist attraction. Leaving West Quoddy Head Light behind, the steamer would have had an easy passage to Cutler. From there, Captain Reed would have aimed for the light at Libby Island (off Bucks Harbor at the entrance to Machias Bay). Actually two islands, Libby Island's first light was built in 1823. It was a simple wooden tower with a brick light-keeper's house nearby. The light tower lasted only a few months before falling down in a storm. Its successor was constructed of stronger beach stone and that was the tower the folks on board would have seen had it been daylight.

The next landfall, ten nautical miles away, was a group of islands off Jonesport, notably Head Harbor and Steele Harbor. Immediately south of Steele Harbor lies tiny Mistake Island and it had a lighthouse at the time called Moose Peak Light. If the visibility was good, the steamer probably next headed directly for Petit Manan, passing to the east of Great Wass Island. The light at Petit

West Quoddy Head Light was a key navigational aid during the *Royal Tar*'s trips between Saint John and Portland. It is located at the easternmost point of the United States, just south of Campobello Island.

Manan, fifteen miles distant, is situated about two miles offshore. Captain Reed would have given it a wide berth because it is surrounded by shallow water.

From Petit Manan, they had a choice of running either to Baker Island Light, off Mount Desert, or to Mount Desert Rock Light. Both are only about fifteen nautical miles from Petit Manan. Again, weather permitting; they could have next headed directly for the light on Matinicus Rock, thirty-six nautical miles away, keeping an eye out for Great Duck and Long Islands. From Matinicus Rock, it was clear steaming for Monhegan, with its light situated on top of the island, about twenty nautical miles distant.

Another twenty miles beyond Monhegan would have taken the *Royal Tar* to the light on Seguin, keeping clear of Damariscove, the Pumpkin Islands and Pumpkin Ledges on the way. Then twenty nautical miles further and they could see the entrance to Portland's harbor. If all had gone well, they would have steamed into the harbor sometime on Thursday morning.

For the steamer's trips to keep on schedule, good weather was quite necessary. If not, the New Brunswick coast offered little in the way of shelter. The same holds true for Maine's coast as far as the Cutler area. From there south, numerous bays and rivers offer a multitude of safe havens that the steamer might have anchored in. Penobscot Bay was such a haven, and in bad weather the *Royal Tar* could have headed for the Fox Island Thorofare between what is now North Haven and Vinalhaven.

In addition to experience with the route and advice from his pilot, Captain Reed most likely had a copy of *The American Coast Pilot* by Edmund and George Blunt on board. Charts of the time were very basic, and the Coast Pilot was the chief means of keeping vessels away from marine hazards. It gave written descriptions only of the courses to follow. For example, a passage reads, "In running from Owl's Head Light (Rockland) for Fox Island thorofare, bring the light to bear west, and steer E. ½ S. until you bring the light on Brown's Head to bear E. N. E., and then steer for it until you are within one cable's length from the light (this is Browns Head Light on Vinalhaven at the west end of the Thorofare). In running this course, you pass between Crabtree's Ledge and Dog Fish Ledge, leaving Crabtree's on the larboard hand, and Dog Fish Ledge on the starboard, which is separated by a channel one mile broad."

Today, you merely turn on a GPS plotter and follow the moving chart to your destination. If it's foul weather or nighttime, just turn on the radar. It is no wonder, with so few navigation aids available at the time, that so many nineteenth-century vessels went aground.

The Engine

On the way home from school, Will likes to stop by the blacksmith shop to see what his father is working on. He enjoys the heat and noise as the men turn iron into something useful for a ship. There are six men, five of them, like his father, from Ireland. John Braxton is bent over an anvil, striking a red-hot piece of iron with a large hammer.

"What's that going to be?" Will asks, moving alongside his father. "It's going to be a keel bolt for the Mechanic, *another ship being built at the same shipyard where the* Royal Tar *was built," answers John. "I'm going to deliver it tomorrow if you want to go. It's Sunday and you don't have school."*

The next day, Will and his father put the new keel bolt, along with several others, in the bottom of a small sailing skiff. Just before slack tide, they start rowing across the harbor to Carleton. Soon a bit of wind is felt and they hoist a single sail and thread their way between an outgoing square-rigged ship and a small schooner making her way from Carleton to the Saint John waterfront. The wind picks up and they make good time across the harbor.

They carry the bolts up the bank to the shipyard. Will wants to look at the work being done on the Mechanic, *a whaling ship, but his father says, "This slack water won't last much longer. We need to get going. We don't want to be late for dinner." Will says, "I hope it's not fish cakes again."*

★   ★   ★

As a means of marine propulsion, the steam age began with Robert Fulton's *The North River Steamboat of Clermont,* later shortened to *Clermont.* The North River referred to the Hudson River. In 1807, the *Clermont,* carrying about forty guests, set out from New York City for Albany, about one hundred and fifty miles north. Snorting and belching her way upriver, she arrived thirty-two hours later, scaring the heck out of people on shore. The same trip by stage-coach took seven or eight days and was a rough and dirty ride. No wonder interest was keen to develop steam power as a practical means of transportation.

When the *Royal Tar* made her trips to and from Portland, the engine that drove her massive paddle wheels was called a vertical walking beam engine. The beam was positioned horizontally on top of a massive "A" frame between the paddle boxes. Large connecting rods led directly down below deck. Its piston, moving up and down, transmitted power to the beam which in turn rocked up and down, much like a seesaw.

The *Royal Tar's* engine, like other early steam engines, was huge and forged of cast iron, which made it extremely heavy. It was pretty basic, consisting of a single cylinder positioned vertically. Inside the cylinder was the piston, about four feet in diameter. The piston was installed upside down with a connecting rod attached to the upper end. This rod extended up through the vessel's deck and was connected to one end of the walking beam. The other end of the beam had a similar connecting rod that went down to the engine room and was bolted to a massive crankshaft, which was fastened to the paddle wheels. As the piston moved one end of the beam up and down, the other end of the beam, likewise moving up and down, transmitted power to the wheels. Both wheels moved in the same direction, either forward or backward. To supply the engine with steam, the *Royal Tar* had two boilers and two fire boxes, feeding two tall smokestacks forward of the walking beam.

This museum model shows the basic parts of a vertical, or walking, beam engine. Steam, from the boilers (7), pushes the piston upward inside the cylinder (1), which pushes up the connecting rod (2) attached to one end of the walking beam (3). The other end of the beam is attached to another connecting rod (4) that pushes down on the crankshaft (5) which turns the paddle wheel (6). The engineer's station (8) is where the engine is operated from. (9) Smaller connecting rod to the air box. (Owls Head Transportation Museum, Owls Head, Maine)

A second, smaller connecting rod led from the forward end of the walking beam down to an air box below deck. This purged the cylinder of unused steam and moved it to the condenser, where it was converted back to water for use in the boilers.

The *Royal Tar*'s engine was built by Fleming, Barlow and Stewart, whose foundry was located on Pond Street in Saint John. After passing through several owners, the business became the Phoenix Foundry in the late 1800s and

The rear of this building in Saint John is believed to be the remains of the Phoenix Foundry, originally the Fleming, Barlow and Stewart Foundry that built the engine for the *Royal Tar*. The foundry finally closed in the mid-nineteen fifties.

continued to do business until about 1955. Their major work was marine and stationary engines, and later locomotive engines. This area of Saint John has been considerably changed, and Pond Street has become Station Street. At least part of the original foundry building today is the site of a popsicle factory.

The cylinder and piston for the *Royal Tar's* engine were extremely heavy, weighing several tons. If they were placed horizontally, like today's engines, the weight of the piston would quickly erode away the lower side of the cylinder. By arranging the cylinder and piston vertically, the wear was spread out around the cylinder, so the engine lasted much longer. Because of the weight of walking beam engines, they were placed as low as possible in the hull to keep the center of gravity low.

This model in the Saint John Museum is most likely what the foundry used to build the engine for the *Royal Tar*. The columns were not used on the steamer but merely serve to support the model. (New Brunswick Museum, Saint John, New Brunswick)

To get the *Royal Tar*'s four foot diameter piston started on its six foot stroke, the engineer worked a starter bar. This long lever, in neutral, stood at the bottom of the engine controls at about a forty-five degree angle. Moving the bar, up or down, caused high-pressure steam, stored in a nearby steam chest, to enter the cylinder through one of two large valves. Once the piston started moving up and down, the valves operated automatically and the starter was disengaged.

One major problem with a walking beam engine occurred if it was shut down and the piston happened to stop at exactly top or bottom dead center. When steam was added to get it moving, it sometimes wouldn't budge in either direction. To solve this, the starter bar was once again called into service. Alternately moving

the bar, up and down, sent steam to both valves. By skillfully working the bar, the engineer could send more steam to one valve or
the other and sometimes get the piston to move. If it was really
locked up, crewmen had to enter a paddle box and using a long
lever kept there for the purpose, turn the paddle wheel itself
enough to get the piston off the dead center position. Then the
engineer could get the engine started properly.

The engineer was stationed near the engine so he could
operate the various bars and levers that kept it running.
Communication with the captain up in the pilot house was via a

Various levers at the engineer's station control the operation of the walking beam
engine. The wall gauge on the right shows
the position of the crankshaft, important
information for starting the engine.
(Shelburne Museum, Shelburne, Vermont)

The Tragedy of the *Royal Tar*

speaking tube or a system of bells. Since the paddle wheels were connected directly to the engine, there was only one way to get the steamer going in the opposite direction. The paddle wheels had to be brought to a complete stop by shutting down the steam flow to the piston. Then the engineer had to get the engine started, but in the opposite direction. This took a great deal of skill and judgment, operating the correct levers and/or bars in the proper order. Occasionally, an engineer would make a mistake and an engine blew up!

The walking beam engine on board the *Royal Tar*, like others

The author points to a boiler sight gauge that indicates how much water is in the boiler. This would play an important role in the story of the *Royal Tar*. (Helen Warner)

of that period, operated slowly, only about twenty to twenty-five revolutions per minute. This propelled her along at somewhere around fifteen or perhaps twenty knots (nautical miles per hour). To maintain enough steam, a cord or two of wood was burned every hour, sending sparks and ashes up the two stacks. They were each quite tall to keep the stuff from raining down on passengers or setting the sails on fire, even when furled. A good part of dockside time was spent moving wood on board and stacking it for use when underway.

Although not the most efficient method of moving a vessel, steam engines and paddle wheels were used throughout much of the nineteenth century. Wood was the principal fuel early on with coal coming into use in the middle of the century. Later engine designs were far more efficient and, combined with screw type propellers, put an end to walking beam engines.

One disadvantage not anticipated with the walking beam engine was the massive weight of the beam itself, located at the top of the "A" frame. If something of great interest occurred on a trip, the passengers might rush to one side or the other of the boat to see what was happening. All that extra weight would cause the steamer to heel and the paddle wheel on that side would get too deep in the water while the other would no longer be immersed. This situation was not efficient and the captain would have to redistribute his passengers or bring the vessel to a stop.

To steer the *Royal Tar*, a conventional rudder was mounted at the stern. It was connected to the steering wheel in the pilot house by ropes that ran below deck and through the engine and boiler room. This arrangement would play a crucial role in the disaster that was coming later that fall.

The Menagerie

It is a Saturday in July. Will and two pals are once again doing what they like best, sitting on the edge of a wharf, watching the activity in the harbor. Will suddenly spots a steamship entering the harbor as she rounds Partridge Island. "Why is she blowing her whistle way out there?" he asks. "Must be something happening. They never sound a whistle that far out." They soon recognize the vessel as the Royal Tar. *The boys hear a band on the steamer start playing and leap to their feet.*

It is Saturday, July 2, 1836. The *Royal Tar* is approaching Saint John after her overnight trip from Portland. As she passes Partridge Island, she begins to slow down. Captain Reed correctly surmises that the docking about to occur will be a memorable one. The steamer slowly approaches the waterfront and a small brass band at the bow begins to play. As Captain Reed maneuvers the *Royal Tar* into position for tying up, a large crowd gathers on the wharf, attracted by the music and the arrival of the steamer. They are astonished to see a huge, gray beast on deck. What can it possibly be and why is it coming to Saint John? As the vessel edges closer, other strange animals can be seen, some tied on deck and others in cages. By the time lines are thrown ashore, the crew can barely move about due to the throng now assembled, everyone craning to see just what the steamer has brought to their city.

What they were seeing, for the first time ever in Saint John,

Partridge Island, situated at the mouth of Saint John's harbor, is the site of the first lighthouse in New Brunswick and the third in all of Canada. The wooden structure, erected in 1791, burned down in 1832, but was immediately replaced. A Quarantine Station on the island handled immigrants who were sick. There are six old graveyards on the island and the remains of military fortifications. (New Brunswick Museum, Saint John, NB W1545)

was a small circus menagerie complete with a magnificent elephant, a tiger, two lionesses, two gnus, a hyena, two dromedaries, six horses, and assorted wagons and cages. In fact, what the people were so excited about was Unit #10 from the Zoological Institute of Boston. It was also known as the Macomber, Welch and Company Menagerie. Traveling with the menagerie was the Burgess Collection of Serpents and Birds, plus a colorful omnibus containing Dexter's Locomotive Museum. The term locomotive had nothing to do with trains but meant that it was a mobile, or traveling, museum. It reportedly contained painted revolving scenes of American cities. There are some

The Tragedy of the *Royal Tar*

Entertainment, as we know it today, was mostly lacking in the early 1800s. Imagination and creativity provided ways to occupy leisure time, as these Saint John River musicians so perfectly illustrate. Although the photograph was taken in the late 1800s, this scene could easily have taken place earlier in the century. (Provincial Archives New Brunswick George Taylor Fonds: P5-479)

references that indicate it may have also included wax figures of prominent Americans.

There was little in the way of entertainment in the late 1700s and early 1800s. Television, movies, radio, and telephones were all in the future. Travel was difficult and people tended to stay in their villages and towns. To fill this need for entertainment, the traveling circus and the smaller menagerie came into being. People loved seeing these strange animals from far-away places. The larger circus generally required a license to operate which was often costly and difficult to obtain. The church especially considered circuses to be morally decadent and run by people of low character. Circuses were ought of as a waste of time and money and were considered incompatible with ordinary pursuits, demoralizing men and corrupting youth. In New England, Connecticut and Vermont banned them altogether.

The smaller menageries were far easier to get licenses for and less expensive to operate. Rather than concentrating on acts, which required performers, a menagerie was basically a collection of wild animals, with perhaps a few simple acts thrown in. One such demonstration might have been a monkey riding around on a horse. Elephants were the most popular attraction, followed by lions and tigers. Serpents were also favorite things to see. The animals were exotic and wild and frightening and they drew enthusiastic crowds whenever a menagerie rolled into town. One of the largest menageries of that period consisted of 36 wagons, 112 horses, 2 elephants, a rhinoceros, a lion, a leopard, a lioness and assorted smaller animals.

Menageries generally carried at least two open sided tents called pavilions. The larger was used for simple acts and may have included a short drama, performed by some of the menagerie's personnel. The smaller pavilion displayed the animals that were kept in cages. Admission was the princely sum of a quarter for the big tent and fifteen or seventeen cents for the smaller.

At the beginning of 1835, there were nine menageries operating in America, and by the end of that year there were thirteen. This would change dramatically the following year when the number of menageries declined to only six. By contrast, the number of circuses jumped to thirteen. There were several reasons for this switch. First, because the menageries were essentially static displays, people were willing to pay to see animals in cages only so many times. Second, circus acts and performers were becoming more exciting and daring. Circuses became larger and more noticeable with gaily painted wagons, larger bands, and bigger tents; and, finally, seating became available. Until then, audiences had to stand around the ring to watch the acts being performed. As railroads expanded, circuses could reach more cities and towns, and many had their own trains to transport all of the equipment, animals, workers, and performers.

Each menagerie was assigned a unit number from one to thirteen. The one that found itself headed for Saint John was Unit #10 from Boston. In order to fit on the steamer, the menagerie was reduced in size. Records are hazy or nonexistent concerning the start of the Unit #10's trip to Canada. There is a mention of it having started in April 1836 at New Rochelle, New York. It was most likely working its way north after spending the winter down south. After New Rochelle, the menagerie set up in Stamford and Norwalk, Connecticut before making its way to Boston. There it probably boarded a steamer for Portland, as there is no record of their stopping anywhere from Connecticut to Boston. At the time, there were two steamers operating between Boston and Portland, the *Independence* and the *Portland*. Unit #10 most likely chose the latter, which sailed on Tuesdays, Thursdays, and Saturdays. The Thursday trip would have had the menagerie connecting with the *Royal Tar*'s Friday evening departure for Saint John.

After arriving in Portland, the menagerie booked passage for Canada, planning on spending the summer in the Maritimes. No menagerie had done this before. In charge was H.H. Fuller; Joshua Burgess ran Burgess's Collection of Serpents and Birds, which included a boa constrictor, a python, two pelicans, and assorted other small animals. He also operated Dexter's Locomotive Museum. In order to make room for all of the menagerie, plus regular passengers, two of the four lifeboats were left behind; they would be retrieved on the next trip to Portland. The decision to leave half the lifeboats would play a significant part in the calamity to come later that year.

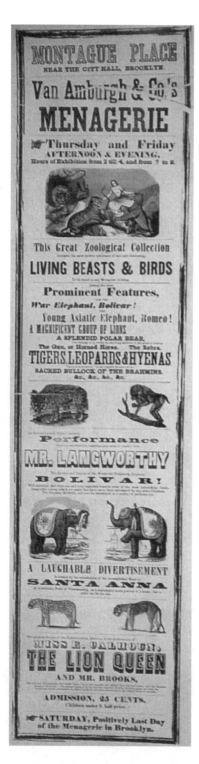

As soon as the gang-plank was down between the *Royal Tar* and Hanford's Wharf, the first person to disembark was most likely someone with an armload of handbills and posters that would be quickly spread around the city. To the delight of the populace, the posters proclaimed that the menagerie would exhibit in Saint John for four days, July 5-8. It must have been unbearably exciting for people to think they would be able to see, up close, all those magnificent and frightening animals that had come from all over the world via America.

Handbills such as this one from the early 1800s, were one of the chief ways to inform the public of a menagerie's date and location. Some had a fill in section where pertinent information could be put as to the time and location of an appearance. (Ringling Museum of Art, Sarasota, Florida)

The Tragedy of the *Royal Tar*

The Maritimes

Will has talked his father into letting him go to the circus exhibition
on the north side of the city. At first, he has difficulty convincing John that
it's a worthwhile thing to do. "When will I ever have another chance to see
wild animals like that again?" Will pleads. "We need every bit of money
we can save to get to America," John says. Will digs in his heels, and says,
"Maybe I can sneak in. A couple of friends are going to try. I can go with
them." John finally relents and gives Will the money. "Thanks!" the boy
squeaks and rushes off.

I t is difficult to say for certain exactly what animals made up the
menagerie that was off-loaded from the *Royal Tar*. Most accounts
vary but some consistency does occur. Therefore, the excited folks
on Hanford's Wharf (or possibly North Market Wharf) that July day
saw a huge elephant walk slowly down a strengthened gangplank,
followed by a gnu. Next were a zebra, two dromedaries, and six
horses. Wheeled cages, containing a Bengal tiger, two lionesses and
assorted smaller animals, including a hyena and an angora goat followed. Also brought ashore were a couple of wagons carrying two
pavilions and the other gear necessary for the menagerie to operate, plus the omnibus.

Once assembled on the wharf, everybody lined up behind
the brass band and the elephant, who was named Mogul. The menagerie then wended its way through the streets of Saint John. It was

headed for a field at the junction of Union and Charlotte Streets at the north end of the city. There the two pavilions were set up for the menagerie's July 5-8 appearances. The larger was used for simple acts, a few animal tricks and a theatrical drama. The omnibus was positioned so people could pass through and admire the changing painted scenes within. One was a fiery view of New York City.

After exhibiting at Saint John, the pavilions were taken down, everything was loaded onto wagons and the menagerie began a summer long tour of the Canadian Maritimes. There were no means of public transportation in those days and walking was the only way to get from one location to the next. The omnibus, wheeled cages and wagons were pulled by the horses, the zebra and the gnu. The dromedaries may have also been enlisted to pull, or at least carry, small loads. Mogul the elephant would have been used when the wagons bogged down in mud or other occasions where his great strength was needed. The menagerie personnel also

Menageries were really exciting events in the early 1800's, as shown by this magazine illustration of a menagerie arriving in town. (The Circus Historical Society, Columbus, Ohio)

The Tragedy of the *Royal Tar*

Crossing rivers such as the Saint John was a problem for the menagerie. There were no bridges in the early 1800s and ferries were the normal means of getting across. Ferries are still an important part of the Canadian transportation system. This modern ferry uses an underwater cable to pull itself across the river.

walked, taking a rest when needed by riding on a wagon for a while.

Getting out of Saint John posed a problem. The short route to Gagetown, the first stop, was about eighty miles to the north. There were no bridges then and the only way across rivers was by ferries. In those days, ferries were large and barge-like in order to carry people, wagons, and horses. It may have taken a few trips, but the menagerie could have easily gotten across the river. They also could have taken a longer route northeast out of Saint John to perhaps Sussex and then turn northwest to Gagetown, a trip of approximately one hundred and fifty miles. Although longer, it would have enabled them to make appearances in towns not on

The Maritimes

When the menagerie arrived in Gagetown, their first stop after Saint John, they would have seen the Tilley House, built in 1786 and birthplace of prominent Canadian politician Samuel Leonard Tilley. The population in 1836, a little over a thousand, was slightly higher than that of today as immigrants from Europe and Loyalists from America arrived and settled in the area. Gagetown was primarily an agricultural and timbering community.

the schedule. There is no record of which way the menagerie went, but it did have two and a half days in which to make it. It is more likely that they crossed the Saint John River by ferry and were able to take the shorter route. A menagerie could move at four or five miles an hour. Traveling for most of the day, and perhaps at night, two and a half days was more than enough time to reach Gagetown. The exhibit was there for only one day, and so the grueling Maritime schedule began.

Their next appearance was at Fredericton, less than a dozen miles away. They probably rested for the night after Gagetown's appearance and set out the following morning. Arriving around noon gave them plenty of time to set up for the two or three days the schedule called for. The exact length of time spent at Fredericton depended upon the crowds. If enough people came they could extend their two day stay. Their schedule for the entire time in the Maritimes was set forth in a route book. They had some flexibility but generally stuck to the plan as, in some cases, advance notices of their arrival had preceded them.

After Fredericton, their next scheduled stop was two hundred and fifty miles to the east, at Truro, in Nova Scotia. Although no stops were planned, they traveled through Moncton and Amherst, both fairly good sized communities. The schedule allowed them a month for the trip so they probably set up there for a day or two and perhaps at other towns along the way as well. After all, they were in Canada to make money, and if time and the weather allowed, they would have made as many interim stops as possible.

After a day or two at Truro, the menagerie set out, probably overnight, for the town of Stewiacke, thirty miles away. This was for a one day exhibit. Then they packed up for another thirty-mile trip to Musquodoboit, again a one day stay. Forty miles southwest was a one day engagement at Gay's River. This was followed by yet another overnight trek to make the fifty miles to Dartmouth, next to Halifax. This seemingly tight schedule, often necessitating travel through the night, was not unusual for menageries. Night was cooler than the hot summer days and made the journey more pleasant. The biggest benefit, however, was that the local population didn't get to see the animals for free as they passed through in the dark.

After the exhibit at Dartmouth, the menagerie made the short trip to nearby Halifax, the capital of Nova Scotia. There, they had a stay of five or six days, and maybe even a little time for relaxation. Unfortunately, there is little newspaper coverage of the time the menagerie spent in Halifax, as a major harbor explosion in 1917 destroyed much of the earlier newspaper records. At the time, the harbor was crowded with World War I shipping traffic. A Norwegian ship, the *Imo,* collided with the *Mont Blanc,* a French munitions vessel. The latter caught fire; the crew abandoned her and she drifted across the harbor where she ended up against a Halifax wharf and then exploded. Many of the city's buildings caught fire and were destroyed. About two thousand people died and thousands more were injured.

After Halifax, the menagerie packed up again and headed for its last scheduled stop, at Yarmouth. From Halifax, they headed inland, northwest across the Nova Scotia peninsula to the eastern shore of the Bay of Fundy. On the way, they made at least sixteen unscheduled stops in towns and villages before reaching Yarmouth on time for the scheduled September 27 engagement. There is an excellent newspaper account of that day. They exhibited from one to four in the afternoon, with the lion keeper entering the cage at three, thrilling everyone with his daring. Here is an excerpt from the *Yarmouth Herald*: "The exercises of the highly trained elephant Mogul — the feeding of the wild beasts — the entering of the Lion's cage and the performances in the ring by the Monkey and Pony — form a truly astonishing and interesting exhibit." The Yarmouth stop ended the schedule posted in the route book for their Maritime visit.

Interestingly, an advertisement in the same newspaper sought a suitable vessel to carry the menagerie to New York after the Yarmouth engagement. It is clear they didn't relish the long trip back to Saint John and were anxious to get back to America for the winter. Unfortunately, no vessel seemed up to the task as no one answered the notice.

The only option was to travel overland back to Saint John, a trip of approximately seven hundred miles. This must have been an unwelcome choice. They had just three weeks to get back before the *Royal Tar's* last scheduled trip to Portland, at the end of

October. This would require walking eight hours each day to cover at least fifty miles. Fair weather would have allowed them to keep to that schedule, but rain, and they no doubt ran into some, changed everything. The only roads were dirt and quickly turned slippery with mud. Deep ruts would have bogged the heavy wagons down, requiring everyone's efforts to get things moving again. Mogul's strength would have been a great asset during those times.

Another consideration was that the menagerie had never been to the Maritimes before, and no one was familiar with the route on poorly marked roads. Local guides helped when available, otherwise someone from the menagerie had to go ahead and scout out the proper way to go.

Because of the necessity of getting back to Saint John before the end of October, the menagerie had no time to stop and exhibit along the way. It was a matter of constantly pushing everybody in order to get there before time ran out. There must have been a great sigh of relief when the menagerie finally crested the hills of

MENAGERIE'S 1836 MARITIMES TOUR ITINERARY

Saint John	July 5–8
Gagetown	July 11
Oromocto	July 12
Fredericton	July 13–16
Truro	August 22–23
Stewiacke	August 24
Musquodoboit	August 25
Dartmouth	August 27
Halifax	Aug 29–Sept 4
Yarmouth	Sept 28–Oct 1

**Taken from the 1836
Zoological Institute
Route Book**

Saint John. They apparently made good time as there is some evidence that indicated they exhibited one more time in the city before setting out for home on the *Royal Tar*. Little did they know what fate had in store for them.

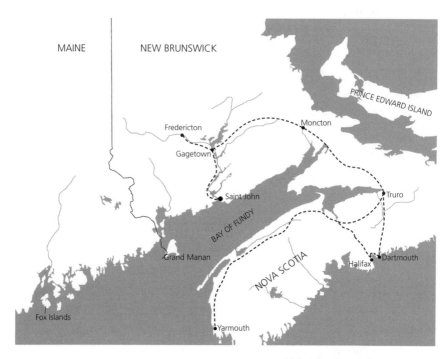

This map shows the route the menagerie took from Saint John to Nova Scotia and back. A one way trip was approximately seven hundred miles, all done on foot. (Erik Hargreaves)

The Tragedy of the *Royal Tar*

Mogul

It is the middle of October and John Braxton has received a letter from his sister, who lives outside Boston. The plan is for him and Will to leave Saint John later in the month on the Royal Tar's *trip to Portland. From there, they hope to book passage for Boston. He has already reserved space on the* Royal Tar.

"What if we can't get to Boston?" asks Will.

"There are several steamers from Portland to Boston," replies John, "we shouldn't have any trouble getting on one."

Will is not happy to be leaving Saint John. He has made some good friends at school and will miss the busy waterfront. John has likewise made friends but realizes that America may be a better place for them, with relatives nearby. They will stay with his sister and her husband until they get settled.

The elephant traveling with the menagerie that summer was named Mogul. There is no question of his popularity, as elephants were the most desirous attraction at both circuses and menageries wherever they went. The first elephant to arrive in the United States was a female from India, who, unlike later elephants, had no name. She was instead referred to as the Crowninshield Elephant, named after Captain Jacob Crowninshield, who acquired her in the Bay of Bengal. He brought her to New York on his ship *America* in April 1796 and sold her to a Mr. Owen for ten thousand dollars. Little

Even though menageries and circuses exhibited exotic animals such as lions and tigers, elephants were the favorite animals.

was known about elephants at the time and at first she was thought to be a male. This first elephant in America was such an unusual sight that her dimensions were given in a handbill advertising her appearance in Boston during the summer of 1797. She measured fifteen feet from the tip of her tail to the end of her trunk. Her girth was ten feet and she weighed three thousand pounds. Male elephants that later arrived in North America proved to be larger. In addition to her regular feed, porter was a favorite drink and she polished off some thirty bottles a day.

In addition to this dark beer, elephants also like any kind of alcoholic beverage and are especially fond of rum.

The Crowninshield Elephant was widely exhibited in Charlestown, Philadelphia, Worcester, Boston, New York, Savannah, Newport, Baltimore, Providence, and in other cities. She traveled and was exhibited alone, with no other animals. There is no record of how long she lived or of her death.

The second elephant arrived in America in 1804 and was named Betty. Like the Crowninshield Elephant, Betty was also a female but she came from Africa. A cattle merchant named Hachaliah Bailey in Somers, New York, bought her to do heavy work on his farm. So many people came to see her that he decided to charge them. He did so well that he started to display her around the northeast and she was soon widely exhibited throughout the eastern part of the country. Like her predecessor, she traveled and was exhibited alone. The price to take a look was twenty-five cents and she was available for viewing from early morning until sunset. A local newspaper advertised her visit to Lexington, Kentucky: "Those who wish to gratify their curiosity by seeing the wonderful works of nature, will do well to call previous to that time (Tuesday the twentieth of December 1808). Perhaps the next generation may never have the opportunity of seeing an Elephant again, as this is the only one in the United States, and perhaps the last visit to this place."

Bet, as she was nicknamed, met an unfortunate end on July 26, 1816, when she was shot and killed by Daniel Davis in Alfred, Maine. He may have had a grudge against the owners or was a staunch Blue Law supporter who thought it sinful to provide entertainment on a Sunday. She had been in America for twelve years and was widely known. Her stuffed remains were exhibited in New York in 1817, and the following year they went on tour. After her death, another elephant was imported in 1817 and was likewise called Betty. To keep the two separate, the first Betty became Old Bet and the newcomer was named Little Bet.

Little Bet was another female elephant and arrived in Boston in December. She was exhibited until her death in 1826. Coincidentally, like Old Bet, she was also shot to death, this time by six men while crossing a bridge in Chepachet, Rhode Island. Apparently, they wanted to test the strength of her hide against musket balls. The men were found guilty and fined $1,500 for damages. Unfortunately, the amount charged was only fraction of the actual value.

Also landed in 1817 was a male elephant named Columbus.

This site in Alfred, Maine, marks the spot where the elephant Betty, later known as Old Bet, was shot and killed in July 1816. Located next to the York County Jail, the marker was donated by the Sanford-Alfred Historical Society.

He was a lone attraction until 1824, when he was shown with other animals in a menagerie. He continued to appear in menageries until his death in 1851. In October, while crossing over the Hoosick River in North Adams, Massachusetts, he fell through the bridge and was badly injured. He died a week later.

The next elephant to arrive in America was Horatio, named for the ship that brought him from India in 1819. Another male, Horatio was exhibited all by himself until he, like Columbus, fell through a bridge. This time it was over the Connecticut River between Putney, Vermont, and Westmoreland, New Hampshire. A short time after, he also died of his injuries.

Another Indian elephant, Tippoo Sultan, arrived in June of

The Tragedy of the *Royal Tar*

1821. He was shown alone until the following year when he was seen with other animals, thus becoming the first elephant to be exhibited as part of a menagerie (Columbus didn't show with other animals until 1824). He stayed with the menagerie for thirteen years, which was billed as the "Grand Caravan with Tippoo Sultan." He went to the West Indies in 1837 and from there left for South America. His last known trip was to Peru in 1840, and there was no further word of him.

In 1827, a female elephant named Flora arrived in Portland, Maine. She did not start out, like her predecessors, as a solo exhibit but was immediately shown along with a camel and a few other animals. She eventually joined a menagerie and seems to have disappeared by 1838.

These early elephants, and others to follow, were

MACOMBER & CO'S

ENTIRE

NEW COLLECTION OF ANIMALS,

CONSISTING of all the principal ANIMALS in America, recently imported from Exeter Change, London, will be exhibited at

MERRILL'S PORTLAND HOTEL,

formerly kept by Mr. Patten, on SATURDAY, July 4,—and for a few days only, afterwards. The Animals in the collection, are as follows:

The Young ELEPHANT, 18 months old only, but 4 feet 6 inches high; the smallness and docility of this little elephant, renders it the greatest curiosity ever offered for exhibition in America. The *Great Polar* or *White Bear*, the only one in America, weighing between 6 and 700 pounds. The full grown *African Lion*, from his full flowing mane and superior carriage, is considered the finest of his species in America. The *Royal Tiger*, imported in the ship Columbia, the 7th inst. from London. Just added, a beautiful *Female Leopard*, with her three young, which were whelped May the 19th, 1829; a curiosity never before exhibited in America. The *Jaguar* is a beautifully spotted animal, and has been often mistaken by naturalists for the tiger. The Hyena is one of the most fierce and bloodthirsty animals that inhabits the Forest.

Also, will be added, the principal Animals in the New England Caravan, viz.—THE MAMMOTH LION, the equal of which the Proprietors defy the world to produce, under a forfeiture of $1000. The African Lioness; Young African Tiger; Panther, or Catamount; Black Wolf; celebrated Dandy Jack & Poney; together with a large collection of different Animals.

The public may rest assured, that every attention will be paid to visiters. The place will be splendidly decorated, & in the evening brilliantly illuminated.

Hours of Exhibition, from 10 o clock A. M. until

An early eighteen hundreds ad in a Portland , Maine newspaper illustrates the importance that elephants had with the public. (Portland Historical Society) often difficult to manage. In general, female elephants were more docile than males, but the latters' larger sizes made them more attractive to paying customers. They could, however, be a handful to control, and there are several instances when they turned on their handlers, badly injuring or even killing them. Pizzaro, in 1845, attacked his keeper and his horse. The horse "was struck with such violence that there was scarcely a bone not broken." Sometime later, Pizzaro again went berserk and attacked a menagerie's animals with such violence that men armed with guns were summoned to subdue him. The elephant received about twenty musket balls, more than half of which were still in him when he died years later. Shortly after this incident, Pizzaro was being coaxed into fording a stream that he just didn't want to cross. No-one else was present, so exactly what happened is not known. The broken bodies of an accompanying camel and the keeper's horse were found nearby. The keeper himself was torn to shreds and parts of him were found thirty feet up in a tree. Pizzaro drowned in 1847, while crossing the Delaware River.

In order to retain control over their charges, elephant keepers resorted to the axiom "fear rules" and they used metal hooks and pitchforks to subdue stubborn elephants. It was not unusual for this practice to cause a good deal of bleeding.

Not all was quite so grim in an elephant's life. They loved flowers and were not shy, on their long treks between engagements, about helping themselves to whatever was available in local gardens. They also liked rum and other alcoholic beverages, especially beer and porter. They also enjoyed eating paper. Handbills of the time warned people not to get too close if they had paper in their hands. They did not like any kind of tobacco and most elephants were, in fact, afraid of mice and rats.

This was the environment that Mogul found himself in when he arrived in the United States. There is very little information on

The Elephant Hotel, in Somers, New York, was built by Hachaliah Bailey in the early 1820's. Often cited as the Cradle of the American Circus, the hotel today serves as the town offices, the Somers Historical Society and the Museum of the Early American Circus. (Terry Ariano)

him except that he arrived in Boston in May of 1831 on the brig *Neponset,* in the company of a small rhinoceros. Mogul was nine years old at the time and he, along with the rhinoceros, was exhibited at the Lion Tavern in Boston. He then ended up as the main attraction in Macomber and Company's New Collection of Living Animals. Mogul made spotty appearances over the next couple of years. Macomber was out of the country during much of 1833 and 1834 procuring animals abroad. The elephant was most likely living at Macomber's farm while he was away.

Mogul reappeared in 1835 when Macomber, Welch & Company became the Boston Unit of the Zoological Institute. At one point, he was even advertised as "The Great War Elephant Mogul." He was on exhibit during 1835 and then, along with the menagerie, boarded the *Royal Tar* for the Maritimes tour in 1836. He was fifteen years old when he died in the tragedy later that fall.

Last Trip

It is Thursday the 20th of October, 1836. John Braxton has gone up King Street to the boarding house where he and Will have been living to say his goodbyes. They have each put one bag on board the Royal Tar. *It is all they have to take south with them. The departure has been delayed because of bad weather, but it looks like she will get off early Friday morning. They will spend the night on board. John is slowly making his way down the hill when he meets an excited Will running up the hill. He has been saying goodbye to some school friends.*

"Pa!" Will shouts. "You won't believe who's going on the boat with us! It's the circus menagerie! All the way to Portland! They're getting on board now!"

Upon returning to Saint John, the menagerie once again set up the pavilions at the same field on the edge of the city. There is no evidence of how long that engagement lasted but it was probably only for a few days. They were eager to leave on the regularly scheduled departure of the *Royal Tar* on Wednesday October 19, but the weather was quite foul and the steamer remained tied to the wharf.

Friday morning, October 21, dawned clear and fair, so loading procedures were begun. This was to be the last trip of the season because of upcoming winter weather and a lack of business. Passengers, freight, and the menagerie were put on board. A large tent was erected over the stern area to shelter much of the menagerie and its equipment. Some of the caged animals were again placed below deck. Mogul the elephant was put in a special stall amidships, over the boiler room. To make room for the menagerie, as on the trip from Portland, two of the four lifeboats were left behind. There were no maritime regulations at the time specifying how many lifeboats had to be carried, so this was not a breach of any safety rules.

When the *Royal Tar* finally left Saint John, there was a crew of twenty-one on board. Thomas Reed was the captain, as he had been all summer. There were about seventy-one passengers on board, including the people of the menagerie. That made a total of ninety-two, but various accounts list anywhere from ninety-two to ninety-six. The actual number will likely never be known. Some reports mention that the pilot's son was on board. Was he included as a passenger or not? Did other members of the crew have any children on board that were not counted? Were the passenger lists of the time just plain inaccurate?

Thirty-four people were listed as having cabin spaces. This number appears the same in all accounts, so it is probably accurate.

East Quoddy Head Lighthouse on the northern tip of Campobello Island marks the way to Eastport. Known locally as Head Harbour Light, the red cross makes the tower easier to see in inclement weather. Erected in 1829, the original wooden structure still stands. (Charles W. Bash)

The Tragedy of the *Royal Tar*

Some members of the menagerie booked cabins and the rest went as steerage. No account was found that listed the exact number of menagerie personnel.

At the time of departure the brass band once again assembled at the bow and began playing. One of the tunes was "God Save The King." Passengers waved to the crowd on the wharf, lines were cast off, and the *Royal Tar* began her fateful voyage into history.

The start of the trip was uneventful. The weather was still clear, but soon a west wind began to blow. Above the noise of the wind in the steamer's rigging, passengers listened to the rhythmic "plosh, plosh, plosh" of the paddle wheels as they turned. By the time the *Royal Tar* reached Eastport for her scheduled stop there, the wind had picked up enough that Captain Reed decided to remain overnight instead of heading directly for Portland.

By the next morning, the wind had increased to near gale strength. The steamer remained in Eastport all day Saturday the 22nd, that night, and into Sunday morning. No doubt the passengers and crew spent time ashore. There would have been a need for extra food for the animals. After all, they should have arrived in Portland on Saturday.

To pass the time, the band may have provided some entertainment and passengers might have done a little dancing. Others sang along with the band. Animals were exercised with the passengers no doubt looking on. Cabin passengers were better off, as they had some privacy, and they had two cooks to provide for them. The wind persisted and Captain Reed was reluctant to leave shelter, so the *Royal Tar* remained in Eastport through Sunday night.

Monday morning, October 24, the wind was still blowing, but Captain Reed decided to try and get farther along. The boiler fires were lit and as soon as steam was up, the *Royal Tar* continued on. The waters are deep along the Maine coast in this area, and they could hug the coast, trying to stay out of the wind, which still

After leaving Eastport, Captain Reed found the going still difficult and put into Cutler for the night. He would have anchored the *Royal Tar* next to or tucked in behind Little River Island.

blew from the west. It was not an easy trip apparently, as Captain Reed put into Cutler for the night. Little River Island sits at the mouth of the harbor and the steamer likely anchored in calmer waters behind it. In the afternoon, rather than staying for the night as planned, Captain Reed once again set out southward. Finding it still windy, and the seas rough, the *Royal Tar* put into Machias Bay and anchored once more. As the evening wore on, the wind shifted to the northwest and began to abate. Captain Reed saw this as his chance to again head for Portland. They were now three days behind schedule and he, like his passengers and crew, was anxious to get under way again.

Around midnight, they weighed anchor and steamed out of

The Tragedy of the *Royal Tar*

An important lighthouse for the *Royal Tar* was that of Petit Manan, roughly half way between Eastport and Penobscot Bay.

the bay. It was dark and visual sightings were difficult. The Maine coast is studded with large and small islands, many ledges and shallow water areas lay ahead. Keeping out of the wind was enough of a challenge, but Captain Reed had made many trips that summer, and he had an experienced pilot on board. Between the two of them, the steamer was navigated through the night. The best help was the series of lighthouses along the Maine coast. The first was Libby Island Light, about five miles from where they had anchored behind Little River Island. Then it was nine miles to Moosepeak Light on Mistake Island. Another run of fifteen miles put them at Petit Manan. Here they had to be especially careful, as the waters are shallow all around the lighthouse. Because of the great hazard to mariners, the light was put up in 1817. It was a crude affair

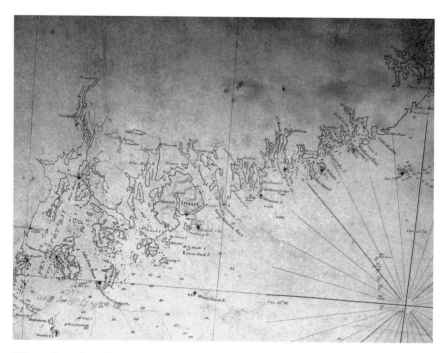

This section of an 1842 Edmund Blunt chart illustrates the Maine coast and the route the *Royal Tar* would have taken one her last trip. Note the lack of detail then available. (Penobscot Marine Museum, Searsport, Maine; www.penobscotmarinemuseum.org)

made up of beach stone but it was the first lighthouse erected between West Quoddy Head and Penobscot Bay.

By the time they passed Baker Island Light and the one on Mount Desert Rock, it was starting to get light, so they could navigate using visual land references. There is no record that shows the route the *Royal Tar* took from those two lights into Penobscot Bay. Because of the strong northwest wind that was still blowing, they needed to get into the shelter of this large bay. Captain Reed had two choices—steam either through Merchants Row or the Deer Island Thorofare. While Merchants Row offered a wider and deeper channel, one

The Tragedy of the *Royal Tar*

account indicates that he instead chose the Deer Island Thorofare. By now, the passengers were up and enjoying the spectacular scenery as the steamer threaded its way through the Thorofare and headed out into Penobscot Bay. It was early afternoon and Captain Reed steered for the shelter of the Fox Island Thorofare, a little over five miles away. Neither he nor his passengers had any inkling of what was about to happen.

Fire!

It is Monday, the 25th day of October. Will and his father are tired and sore from sleeping on the hard deck. As steerage passengers, they have no cabin but were given a blanket each. They have found a sheltered spot but it has been three days now since leaving Saint John. The Royal Tar *spent a couple of days at Eastport and John and Will went ashore several times. The wife of their boarding-house owner had given them a loaf of bread and some cheese for the overnight trip to Portland but that is all gone. They are glad the steamer is finally moving south again. Will is spending as much time as he can among the animals. He is very excited when one of the menagerie men allows him to help feed the tiger.*

hen the *Royal Tar* steamed into Penobscot Bay, she was entering the largest such body of water in Maine. Fifteen miles wide and forty miles long (running north and south), Penobscot Bay is dotted with more than two hundred islands. The largest are Deer Isle, Islesboro, North Haven, and Vinalhaven. At the time, the latter two were known as North Fox Island and South Fox Island, with the Fox Island Thorofare separating them. The Thorofare is about five miles long and offers a multitude of good anchorages. It is there that Captain Reed and the *Royal Tar* was headed when she entered the Bay late on Tuesday morning, the twenty-fifth day of October 1836.

The northwest wind was still blowing hard down the bay and

Captain Reed steered for the lee of the Fox Islands and the shelter offered by the Thorofare. There are many diverse reports, accounts and speculation as to exactly what happened as the *Royal Tar* approached the Fox Islands. All accounts agree, however, that one or both boilers were running out of water. As the steam pressure dropped, Captain Reed was informed of the situation and decided to drop anchor in order to check the water in the boilers. It was now about one-thirty in the afternoon and the steamer was located approximately a mile east of Bluff Head, at the northeastern tip of South Fox Island (Vinalhaven). The boiler water situation was now investigated.

To determine the amount of water in a ship's boiler, someone looks at a glass sight gauge located at the end of the boiler, above the fire box. This glass tube is mounted vertically, and the water level can be clearly seen in the tube. If however, the boiler is full, there would be no water line, as it would be above the top of the gauge. Likewise, if it were empty, the level would be below the visible portion of the tube. In that situation, it could be wrongly interpreted that the boiler was full.

Most reports state that someone told the second engineer that a boiler (or both), was empty. Some accounts say it was the pilot's son who reported this, others claim a passing crewman. In any event, all reports say that the second engineer, Mr. Kehoe, claimed to have told that crewman, or a fireman, to take care of it. The senior engineer, Mr. Marshall, was asleep at the time, as he had been up all the previous night dealing with an engine problem, so Mr. Kehoe was in charge. There was some sort of communication problem and, in fact, no one had filled the boilers which quickly overheated.

When Mogul the elephant was put aboard in Saint John, a special stall was built for him on deck over the boiler room. There was little room between the deck beams and the tops of the boil-

A boiler sight gauge similar to that on the *Royal Tar.* The water level would show in the glass tube. (Shelburne Museum, Shelburne, Vermont)

ers, so wooden wedges were driven into the spaces to add support for the weight of the elephant above. Shortly after the *Royal Tar* came to anchor, the wedges burst into flame and fire quickly spread out under the wooden deck above. Soon, smoke began billowing up from the engine room vents, and that caught people's attention. Captain Reed immediately sent crew members below to deal with the situation.

Unfortunately, the only fire-fighting equipment on board was located in the very space where it was needed the most. The thick smoke soon forced the crew to abandon the boiler room, leaving the fire to spread out of control. With no effective way to fight the

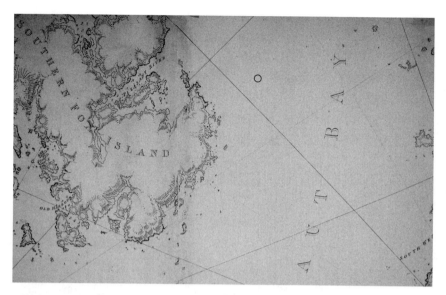

The circle marks the approximate spot where the *Royal Tar* caught fire. Southern Fox Island is now called Vinalhaven. (Penobscot Marine Museum, Searsport, Maine; www.penobscotmarinemuseum.org)

fire, Captain Reed ordered the anchor line severed and the jib and mainsail raised. He was trying to get the steamer to shore and beach her. Just as they were getting underway, the fire burst through a forward hatch and sparks quickly set the sails on fire. At the same time, the rudder cables (actually ropes) running from the pilot house, through the boiler and engine room, caught fire and burned through, crippling the vessel. The *Royal Tar* was now at the mercy of the fire.

At this point, the second engineer, and fifteen others (both crew and passengers), put the larger of the two lifeboats overboard and jumped in. They quickly put out oars and headed downwind for Isle Au Haut, some six miles away. There was speculation that this was a cowardly act and they were attempting to save only themselves. After all, the bigger lifeboat could have held many more people if they had been able to get on board. Another explanation,

The Tragedy of the *Royal Tar*

though, might be that they hadn't actually intended to immediately set out for Isle Au Haut, but once cast off found they couldn't bring the heavy lifeboat around after moving out from under the lee of the *Royal Tar*. The wind and rough seas proved to be too much for them and their only choice was to continue on to Isle Au Haut. In any event, the sixteen safely reached their destination some four hours later. Although vilified in many accounts, there is no record that the second engineer was ever brought up on any charges.

With the steamer now blazing in several areas, Captain Reed ordered the jolly boat, the smaller of the two lifeboats, put over the side. He, and two others, jumped in and started after the other lifeboat, headed for Isle Au Haut. They couldn't, however, catch up and soon managed to turn the jolly boat around and headed back to the burning steamer. As they neared the *Royal Tar*, a man from the menagerie leaped over, swam to Captain Reed's boat, and was pulled aboard.

By now, the steamer was burning furiously. The horses had been backed over the side and were frantically swimming around the stricken vessel. Some of the other deck animals were also put over to fend for themselves. These would have been the gnu, the camels, and the zebra. Unfortunately, the caged animals, some on deck and some below, were not let out. It was feared that, in their panic, they would be more deadly to the passengers and crew than the fire and the sea. By that time, most of them had probably, mercifully, succumbed to the smoke.

Although Mogul was set free from his stall, he refused all attempts to get him to abandon ship, instead moving from one area to another in an attempt to escape the flames. The crew and passengers, now left to fend for themselves, likewise ran from the fires until there was no place left to go. Some jumped directly into the sea. Others climbed over the side and clung to ropes or hung on various parts of the hull, including the rudder. Several men quickly constructed a crude raft of whatever they could find that would float and pushed it over the side. It began to look like very few would survive, but then people began shouting. At first, many must have thought they were seeing a mirage. Through the smoke and flames, they spotted a small, fully rigged schooner, drawing rapidly near. Perhaps, they might survive after all.

Rescue

"Will! Where are you?" John Braxton cannot see his son with all the smoke and ash flying around on the burning Royal Tar. *They became separated when Will went to help get one of the horses over the side. The wind is howling in what is left of the ship's rigging. The roar of the fire makes it impossible to hear anything else. People are screaming everywhere.*

Suddenly, Will appears at John's side. His face is smudged with soot. "We got all the horses over," he shouts. John has found a piece of stout rope and ties one end around a section of railing and throws the other end over the side. He has also tied some knots and put a loop near the bottom.

"Quick!" John yells. "Over the side!" "Don't let me fall," Will shrieks. "I can't swim!"

The vessel seen bearing down on the *Royal Tar* through the smoke and fire was the small Revenue Service Cutter *Veto*. She had been in the vicinity, spotted the smoke and headed for the stricken steamer as fast as she could under the conditions. The *Veto* was under the command of Captain Howland Dyer, a Fox Island resident who knew the waters well. By this time, the fire had been burning for about half an hour and the *Royal Tar* was in desperate straits. Smoke and flames were everywhere. The few sails that had been set had burned away, as had the rudder cables. The anchor line had been cut so Captain Reed could try to get the steamer to nearby South Fox Island and beach her. There was no steam in the boilers. The *Royal Tar* was at the mercy of the elements and drifting downwind to the southeast.

By now, the deck animals that had been put over the side were struggling in the water. Reports later stated that the horses swam around and around the steamer until, exhausted, they one by one sank below the surface. Mogul, who had by now refused to jump overboard, had no place left to escape the fire and was beginning to get singed. In a panic, he put his front feet up on a railing, hesitated, and then plunged overboard. Several accounts claimed he landed squarely on the make-shift raft that had been put overboard, bursting it apart and drowning some of its occupants. In any event, Mogul decided not to stick around and struck out downwind, finally disappearing from sight.

At this point, the *Royal Tar* was completely on fire amidships. Those people still on board were congregated either at the bow or stern. As the flames crept toward them, they too leaped into the cold water. Some were able to swim back to the steamer and grab hold of ropes dangling over the side. Others, who either couldn't swim, or make headway against the waves and wind, quickly sank into the sea. The lucky ones could only clutch those already hanging from the steamer. Captain Reed, in the jolly boat, kept his distance as he was afraid that if he let any more people on board, the small boat would capsize.

This was the scene when Captain Dyer brought his cutter close to the burning *Royal Tar*. His schooner had a large amount of gunpowder on deck for her guns, and he was reluctant to get too near the burning steamer for fear of setting the powder off. He apparently did, however, make an attempt to get close enough to take some passengers off, but sparks started a few small fires on the *Veto*. He managed to get away before any serious fires erupted. The small flames were easily extinguished, although Captain Dyer himself suffered a few minor burns.

This painting depicts the situation about half an hour after the fire started. The Revenue Cutter *Veto* has just arrived and is seen in the background. Captain Reed, in the black hat, is picking up passengers to transfer them to the *Veto,* and some passengers still cling to the burning *Royal Tar.* (Acrylic on prepared wood panel by Stephen Busch)

Keeping his schooner nearby, Captain Dyer sent his pilot to the steamer in their small lifeboat. Frantically rowing in the wind and seas, the pilot was afraid to get close and people clinging to the *Royal Tar* refused to let go of whatever they clung to. After passing around the stern of the steamer, where some fifteen people clung to the rudder and its chains, he managed to get back to the *Veto.* At this point, Captain Reed ordered his small crew of three to row to the cutter, but they refused, claiming it would be too difficult in the rough seas. The captain reputedly yelled, "I was captain of the big boat and damn me if I'll not be of the small one. If any man refuses to do as I say, I'll throw him overboard." The men quickly rowed over to the *Veto.*

After his passengers were transferred, Captain Reed rowed

Rescue

back to his steamer, and again keeping away, but staying as close as he dared, held out an oar to aid those passengers willing to swim to him. After filling the jolly boat, he again rowed back to the cutter. Several trips later, he became exhausted and was relieved at the oars by Mr. Brown, the *Royal Tar*'s steward. Eventually, sixty of the passengers and crew made it to the *Veto*. A total of thirty-one had drowned; one elderly woman is reported to have burned to death. An interesting incident involved one of the passengers that drowned. He apparently fancied himself a strong swimmer, so he bound five hundred dollars in silver coin around his waist and leaped over the side. He, unfortunately, with that extra weight, went straight to the bottom of Penobscot Bay. Neither he nor his money was ever seen again.

H. H. Fuller, the manager of the menagerie, had been seasick in his cabin bunk and awoke to hearing a great deal of commotion. He realized that he was alone in the cabin and rushed outside to see what was happening. He found the vessel aflame and managed to get to the stern rail where "my coat took fire. I looked around, and seeing not a soul around me in the boat, I fastened a rope to the tiller chain, and dropped over the stern, where I found about fifteen others hanging in different places, mostly in the water. In fact, the water washed over all of us almost every minute. While holding on, I saw several drown—some were beaten from their hold by the waves, and some falling into the sea for want of strength to sustain themselves any longer. I had fastened my rope to the chain, which was fastened by iron bolts, which held out against the fire much longer than the other parts to which many were suspended. I wound the rope around my neck and thigh and was enabled to bear up the additional weight of three men and a lady who hung securely to me. Not far, hung Captain Atkins the Pilot— he held up a lady with his foot; her arms failed her at last, but he caught her head with his feet, and held her for full five minutes, till she washed off and she drifted by; a kind wave washed her up against an Irishman hanging on my left, and she seized hold of him, and assisted, perhaps by our encouraging, and the Irishman's also, kept up." They were all eventually rescued by Captain Reed or Steward Brown in the jolly boat.

When it was believed that all who could be saved had been, Captain Dyer was ready to get the survivors to land. One of the rescued, a William Majoram, acting on his own, persuaded Captain Reed to allow him to take the *Royal Tar*'s jolly boat back for one last look. He, accompanied by one of the other survivors, rowed back to the burning steamer and, "on reaching the wreck there was one woman holding on the bowsprit with a child in her arms, and another in the water with her clothes burnt off, holding on by a piece of rope; she let go and drowned before I could get to her; as did the child, but we saved the woman who was nearly dead—but after using the means that is usually adopted, she revived." (One report stated that the two women were sisters).

S. Patten, a cabin passenger, described how Mogul resisted all attempts to get him off the steamer. "Neither force nor any other means could induce him to follow, and he remained, poor fellow, viewing the devastation, until the fire scorching him, he sprang over the side, and was seen striking out lustily for shore, his trunk held high in the air." (There was no mention of him crushing a raft).

Of the thirty-two people lost from the *Royal Tar*, five were cabin passengers, twenty-four were steerage passengers and three were crew members. Four of those lost were members of the menagerie. Although rumors and stories persisted for many years after the tragedy, none of the animals from the menagerie survived. Mogul's body was later seen floating near Brimstone Island, off the southern end of South Fox Island (Vinalhaven).

After the rescue of the woman from the bowsprit, the *Veto* sailed downwind for Isle Au Haut. Landing there about eight in the

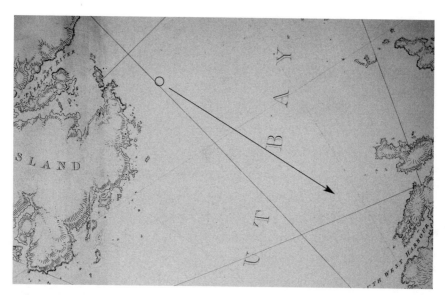

Rescued passengers and crew from the *Royal Tar* were taken to Isle au Haut, across Penobscot Bay from Vinalhaven. (Penobscot Marine Museum, Searsport, Maine; www.penobscot-marinemuseum.org)

evening, the survivors were taken in and cared for by the inhabitants. The next day, October 26th, a small fishing schooner took most of the survivors across a now calmer Penobscot Bay to Rockland. There they transferred to the steamer *Bangor*, where Captain Samuel Howes gave them, "very kind and gentlemanly treatment."

Captain Reed, on the same day, wrote a letter to Leonard Billings, steamboat agent at Portland. Part of his statement follows: "I have no blame to attach to anyone—I think that it was pure accident. I am very stiffened by overexertion, but hope to be better shortly. The people here have been very kind, indeed, and we are as well off as can be expected." Those survivors that remained on Isle Au Haut, including Captain Reed, traveled back to Saint John on the schooner *Ploughboy*, out of Eastport.

The Tragedy of the *Royal Tar*

The *Veto*

Will and John have been hanging on their rope for what seems like a long time. John is sitting in the loop he put in the end and both he and Will hold onto the line with death grips. They have seen several exhausted people let go of what they were hanging onto, quietly disappearing beneath the waves. The horses and other animals have also succumbed. Mogul swam away and they don't know what has happened to him. Both Will and John have seen the revenue cutter Veto *sail around the* Royal Tar, *once very close, but no one from the steamer was able to get on board the schooner. John is beginning to wonder how much longer they can hang on. It is cold and they are wet from spray and waves washing over them.*

"Pa, look!" cries Will, pointing toward the stern of the Royal Tar. *Coming around the steamer is a small rowboat with Captain Reed and a couple of other people on board. They draw near and Captain Reed shouts, "Let go and swim to us!" Will says to his father, "I can't swim. What can I do?" John replies, "Just hang onto me. You'll be fine." Will wraps himself around his father's neck and John slips out of the loop. Quickly swimming to the small boat, John grabs an oar and they are pulled on board.*

The vessel that was instrumental in the saving of so many lives from the *Royal Tar* was the small United States Revenue Cutter *Veto*, based in Castine, Maine. She had been on routine patrol, happened to be in Penobscot Bay that day in late October, and the captain had spotted the smoke from the burning steamer.

When George Washington was sworn in as the nation's first president, he faced a multitude of problems. Spain and Great

Britain still occupied some American territory, the west was threatening secession, his army was small, and there was no navy at all. Goods flowing into the new country from overseas were subject to a tariff, the only way the new government could raise revenue. To avoid this tariff, smuggling had become extremely popular. Washington created the position of Secretary of the Treasury and appointed Alexander Hamilton to run it. Hamilton immediately established a network of customs collectors up and down the Atlantic coast. The problem was that the collectors had no way of acquiring the tariffs as incoming ships by-passed them. In 1790, Hamilton went before Congress and proposed a U.S. Revenue Cutter Service; its mission would be to collect tariffs for the customs collectors.

Congress passed Hamilton's bill and the way was clear for the construction of ten vessels, each following a common design. The bill included a provision that the cost for each vessel couldn't exceed one thousand dollars. If a state went over budget, it had to come up with the extra funds.

The first Revenue Service vessel to be completed was the *Massachusetts,* built by the Serle & Taylor shipyard in Newburyport and launched in 1791. At sixty feet, she was larger than the other nine as she was beefed up to cope with winter patrols in New England. Because of this, she ran considerably over budget and the state of Massachusetts had to come up with an extra thousand dollars. Her crew consisted of a captain, three other officers, and six enlisted men, some of whom were marines. She was armed, like most of the original cutters, with only small arms. Later revenue vessels were outfitted with small swivel guns, firing four or six pound cannon balls.

By early 1793, all ten revenue cutters were on station up and down the eastern seaboard. One each was placed in Massachusetts, New Hampshire, Long Island Sound, New York, the Bay of

The sixty foot long Revenue Cutter *Massachusetts* was the first of ten revenue cutters authorized by Alexander Hamilton. Launched in 1791, she was the biggest of this group. Although rigged as a schooner, she was still referred to as a cutter. (United States Coast Guard)

Delaware, North Carolina, South Carolina and Georgia. Two were assigned to the Chesapeake Bay.

Those first ten vessels, and many subsequent ones, were mostly schooner rigged (two masts with the shorter one forward) but were still referred to as cutters. The word originated in Great Britain and meant "a small, decked ship with one mast and bowsprit, with a gaff mainsail on a boom, a square yard and topsail, and two jibs and a staysail." By general use, cutter came to mean any vessel in Great Britain's Royal Custom Service. The term was adopted by the U.S. Treasury Department for its vessels in the new Revenue Service.

Just when the first ten cutters came into service, France declared war on Great Britain and Spain. Because of America's alliance with Great Britain, French privateer vessels entered American ports and interfered with American shipping. Since the Revenue Service had the only armed vessels, they were called upon to prevent this intervention by France. Despite this extra duty, the cutters were still required to enforce the collection of tariffs, and prevent the ever popular smuggling operations. Then another new task was thrust upon them—charting harbors and rivers. There were not many aids to navigation in the early 1800s and those in existence were maintained by the revenue service. It was also given the job of establishing new lighthouses along the coast.

During the War of 1812, revenue cutters joined the new U.S. Navy fighting Great Britain's warships. Shortly after the war, piracy by Caribbean vessels became a serious problem along the east coast. Revenue cutters now had additional battles to fight. Older cutters were not up to the task, so larger vessels began to be added to the service. In 1893, in an effort to aid stricken mariners, the Life Saving Service was created and established a series of life saving stations along the eastern seaboard. The Revenue Service and the Life Saving Service were merged in 1915, becoming the United States Coast Guard.

In the early days of the Revenue Service, the northeast coast was not regularly patrolled in winter. In 1830, Portland's customs collector ordered the revenue cutter *Detector* to establish regular patrols as far east as Passamaquoddy Bay in northern Maine. She was also to patrol as many rivers and harbors in between as possible. The *Detector,* like most other revenue cutters, had a design that did not function well in winter, and ice became a major problem. Like all cutters, she had heavy masts and accumulating ice soon rendered her dangerously top heavy. She often had to head into a sheltered area and her crew put to work chipping ice from the rigging and masts. Obviously, it was time for a vessel that could remain on patrol all year long in New England, especially in the northernmost sector of Maine.

To fill this need, the *Veto* was built, in 1832, by a shipyard in Blue Hill, Maine. She was specially designed to cope with the difficulties of winter. One of the smaller cutters, she was only forty-nine feet in length on deck, with a beam of thirteen feet and drew seven feet. She was rigged as a topsail schooner with gaff mainsail and foresail. Her foremast also sported a square topsail. She had a bowsprit and could carry two jibs. Her crew was listed as being nine, but there are some reports that she was sailing short-handed when she came to aid of the *Royal Tar*.

Except for her timely appearance on that fateful day in October 1836, the *Veto* had an uneventful career. There is very little else written about her, and she was eventually sold in 1850.

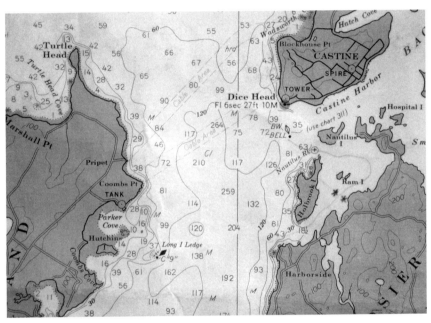

Castine, where the *Veto* was stationed, lies just north of Cape Rosier. The island to the lower left is the northern tip of Isleboro. Castine is almost twenty miles from where the *Royal Tar* caught fire. (Coast Geodetic Survey Chart, 1968)

Epilogue

n 1962, two sea urchin divers working in Penobscot Bay found what appeared to be a melted winch and a piece of charred rudder. These objects were located between Vinalhaven and Deer Isle. A local historian is convinced that these items were from the *Royal Tar*. The hull itself has never been located.

Surviving passengers and crew escaped the burning steamer with their lives and little else but the clothes they were wearing. To better understand their plight, this small announcement was placed in Portland's *Eastern Argus* of November 7th, 1836:

> A man and two female passengers who were on board the *Royal Tar* at the time of her destruction by fire, have arrived in this city, in destitute circumstances, on their way to Boston, for which place they leave in the steamboat on Monday evening. In the meantime, they will be thankful for any assistance which the benevolent may be pleased to grant them, in this city. Donations left at this office will be paid to the sufferers previous to their departure.

Sailors, especially those of the nineteenth century, were a superstitious lot. It was bad luck to have a woman on board. Hulls were not to be painted blue (that color was reserved for Poseidon). There were many other superstitions; one reinforced by the *Royal*

Tar tragedy—it was bad luck to sail on a Friday. Due to delaying weather, the *Royal Tar* did not leave Saint John on her fateful voyage on the scheduled Wednesday, but instead left on a Friday morning.

Public interest in the *Royal Tar* tragedy continued for a long time after the disaster. A "Moving Diorama" was advertised in the Portland newspapers that, in two hundred square feet of canvas, showed "smoke and flames, which are continually moving, ascend obliquely to the left of the picture, being driven fiercely by the wind. The boat, which is in the distance, rises and falls with each succeeding wave; her masts are seen to fall and parts occasionally caving in, yielding to the elements. The small boats supposed to contain those saved are discovered during the scene, rowing in different directions, the figures moving in such a manner as to represent real life." Apparently large crowds came to Portland's Union Hall for six weeks to see this show and "were suitably impressed."

Shortly after the loss of the *Royal Tar*, a joint stock company was formed in Saint John to find a replacement for the steamer. The goal was to have service restored by the spring of 1837. The Canadian steamer *Gazelle* was chosen and made trips to Eastport and Windsor, Nova Scotia. She was lost after striking a ledge only thirty miles from Saint John. There was no loss of life, but passengers and crew barely made it off before she sank.

In March of 1838, a new steamer, the *Nova Scotia,* began service between Saint John, Eastport, and a few other destinations. Her new captain was Thomas Reed.

Despite rumors that Mogul the elephant was seen munching hay in a farmer's field, the sad truth is that he drowned. His body was spotted in the vicinity of Brimstone Island a couple of days after the fire. A large leg bone was later found washed up on the eastern shore of Vinalhaven and reportedly came into the ultimate possession of Edward Rowe Snow's daughter. Mr. Snow was the author of several books on marine disasters.

Several men from Vinalhaven managed to salvage the anchor from the *Royal Tar* and reportedly sold it for four hundred dollars.

There were rumors, and even a newspaper account, that Captain Howland Dyer was not actually on board the revenue cutter at the time, but they were proven false. The newspaper later reprinted a retraction. The Saint John *Observer* newspaper reported that "Thomas Reed, Master of the late steamer *Royal Tar*, begs to tender his sincere thanks to Captain Howland Dyer, commanding the United States cutter *Veto*, and his crew, for their great exertions in saving the survivors from the Steamer, when on fire in Penobscot Bay, on the 25th of October."

Captain Reed himself, in November of 1836, was presented with a purse of seven hundred dollars, raised by survivors, for his role in saving them from the *Royal Tar*. After commanding the steamer *Nova Scotia,* he was appointed Harbor Master of Saint John. He later retired in the same city and died in August 1860. He was sixty-nine years old.

Steward Brown, who relieved Captain Reed on the jolly boat oars when transferring survivors to the *Veto,* was presented with a purse of one hundred and forty dollars.

In an especially cruel turn of fate, Captain Reed's eight year old son, William Grant Reed, after an illness of only forty-eight

The grave marker for Captain Thomas Reed and his family in the Fernhill Cemetery. Located on Westmorland Road, Saint John, Fernland was established in 1848 as the Rural Cemetery; the name was changed to Fernhill in 1899.

hours, died on the very day the *Royal Tar* burned. He was buried a few hours after his father's return to Saint John.

Captain Howland Dyer left the *Veto* in 1843 and became the lighthouse keeper at Browns Head Light, at the western entrance to the Fox Island Thorofare. He remained at that post until 1860. Dyer died 11 January, 1870 and is buried in Browns Head Cemetery on Vinalhaven.

Despite rumors that some animals from the *Royal Tar* reached shore, in fact none did. There is, however, an account of a Bengal

Browns Head Light, at the western end of the Fox Island Thorofare. After leaving the *Veto*, Captain Howland Dyer was lighthouse keeper there for twenty-six years.

tiger roaming the coast of Maine in 1850, fourteen years after the steamer burned. Apparently a vessel carrying another menagerie burned and sank between Machias and Ellsworth. The tiger escaped his cage and made it to shore. After wandering around for a month or two, it settled in the area of Surrey (near Blue Hill), where it lived off the local livestock. One night it was seen in the woods by a man named Black, but few believed his story. The local pastor decided that Mr. Black had had too much rum that night and held a Sunday service intended to point out the dangers of imbibing liquor. Before he could begin, a woman burst through the church doors claiming she was being chased by a tiger! The congregation rushed outside, where they saw

The day after the tragedy, most of the survivors were taken to Rockland, entering the harbor past Owls Head Light (built in 1825 and rebuilt shortly after the *Royal Tar* fire).

the animal emerging from the nearby woods. Mr. Black, who at the time of his sighting was, in fact, sober, had the foresight to ring the church bell. The tiger, upon hearing this strange sound, stopped his charge and retreated back into the trees. The men rushed home for weapons and dogs. They eventually cornered the tiger, but retreated when threatened by its loud roar. One of the men had brought a twenty-five pound whale gun that fired an explosive shell. He managed to hit the tiger in the shoulder, where the shell exploded and blew the poor animal to bits, except for its head, which was presented to Mr. Black.

After the *Royal Tar* disaster, H. H. Fuller, the manager of the menagerie, returned to the Maritimes the following summer with another menagerie called the "Boston Amphitheater." He also returned in 1838 for a last tour. The rise in popularity of the larger circus had put an end to most of the smaller menageries.

The cost of the *Royal Tar* was around fifty thousand American dollars and she was not insured. A like amount of money, perhaps more, was estimated to have been on board, representing the take from the Maritime tour. The value of the lost menagerie, including wagons, two pavilions and other equipment, plus luggage and personal items belonging to the passengers and crew, added another hundred thousand to the loss. Mogul's value was fifteen thousand dollars.

Following the *Royal Tar* tragedy, the survivors from Saint John got together every year for dinner on the 25th of October. By 1896, all of them had died except one, W. H. Harrison of Sackville, New Brunswick. He was interviewed by the Saint John *Telegraph* concerning his time on the burning steamer. He had been one of the fifteen hanging on the rudder. When he gave his account to the *Telegraph,* Mr. Harrison was eighty-four years old.

Every tale has an ending and the story of the *Royal Tar*, at least for the time being, ends here. Unfortunately, there are many questions that most likely will remain unanswered. There are, of course, no living survivors. Missing and destroyed records, plus the passage of more than a century and a half are also to blame. Her whereabouts remain a mystery, but the *Royal Tar* surely lies somewhere on the ocean floor, perhaps one day to be discovered?

John and Will Braxton landed in Portland, like other survivors, with nothing except their clothes. John had put some of their meager savings into his pockets before climbing over the side of the Royal Tar. *It was not much, but it was enough for them to book passage on a steamer for Boston. There, they are living with his sister and her husband until they can find their own place. John quickly found work at the Charlestown Navy Yard and is happy to be working with iron again. Will is doing well at school, has made new friends, and is finally learning to swim.*

Bibliography

Adams, Herbert. "The Day a Floating Circus Came to Grief," *Portland Sunday Telegram,* November 3, 1991.

Atlas of Saint John, City and County, New Brunswick. Saint John, NB: Roe & Colby, 1875.

Bachelder, Peter D. "Penobscot Bay Disaster." *Portland Evening Express*, October 1, 1966.

_____. *Shipwrecks & Maritime Disasters of the Maine Coast.* Portland, ME: The Provincial Press, 1997.

Beveridge, Norwood P. *The North Island Early Times to Yesterday.* North Haven, ME Historical Society, 1976.

Blake, Ruth. "The Loss of The Royal Tar," *The Maritime Advocate and Busy East,* September 1950.

"Burning of the Royal Tar." *The Vinalhaven Neighbor*, October 19, 1938, Vol.1, No.48.

Canfield, Clark. "Expert thinks relics are of circus ship that sank off coast." *Portland Press Herald*, September 21, 1992.

Canney, Donald L. *U.S. Coast Guard and Revenue Cutters, 1790–1935.* Annapolis, MD: Naval Institute Press, 1995.

Charlebois, Peter. *Sternwheelers & Sidewheelers, The Romance of Steamdriven Paddleboats in Canada.* NC Press Limited, Toronto, 1978.

Chilles, Bill. "The Burning of the Royal Tar." Impartial Fulfillment of the Requirements for World Geography for Mr. Pederson May 6, 1983.

"Conflagration of the Royal Tar". *Connecticut Courant,* November 26, 1836.

Crowe, Mike. "Between a Rock and a Hard Place." *Fisherman's Voice,* January, 1999.

"Dreadful Calamity." *Saint John Observer,* November 1, 1836, Vol. IX, No. 18.

"Dreadful Catastrophe." *Eastern Argus,* Vol. 2, No. 257, October 29, 1836.

"Dreadful Disaster—Steamer Royal Tar Burnt: Thirty-two Lives Lost.*" Courier Gazette,* October 29, 1836.

Fuller, H. *Eastern Argus,* Saint John, NB. November 4, 1836, Vol. 2 #262.

Gordon, John. *The Burning of the Royal Tar.* Vinalhaven, ME: Gordon Press, 1886.

"Great Attraction." *Yarmouth Herald,* Yarmouth, Nova Scotia. September 16,
    1836.

Greenhill, Basil. *The Evolution of the Wooden Ship.* U.K.: B.T. Batsford Ltd. 1988.

Gross, Clayton H. "Thanksgiving Tiger Hunt," *AAA Northern New England,* Vol.5, No.6 November/December 1999.

"History of Somers," www.somersny.com, May 6, 2008.

Hocking, Charles. *Dictionary of Disasters at Sea During the Age of Steam.* London, U.K.: Lloyd's Register of Shipping, 1969.

Howland, Southworth A. *Steamboat Disasters and Railroad Accidents in the United States.* Spooner & Howland, 1940.

Hughes, Pat. "Tiger Hunt Escaped Circus Animal Terrorizes Surry." *Discover Maine (Hancock County),* 2000.

Johnson, Arthur L. "The International Line: A History of the Boston-Saint John Steamship Service." *The American Neptune,* Vol. 33, No. 2, April 1973.

King, Irving H. *The Coast Guard Under Sail.* Annapolis, MD: Naval Institute Press, 1989.

Lewis, James A. *The Pilot Yearbook,* North Haven, Maine, 1931

McLane, Charles B. *Islands of the Mid-Maine Coast: Penobscot and Blue Hill Bays.* Kennebec River Press, 1982.

Marestier, Baptitiste J. *Memoirs on Steamboats of the United States of America.* The Royal Press, Paris, 1824.

Marsters, Roger. *Shipwreck Treasures: Disaster and Discovery on Canada's East Coast.* Formac Publishing, 2002.

Morrison, J. H. *History of Steam Navigation.* W. F. Samitz & Company, New York, 1903.

New Brunswick Magazine, Vol. 1, No. 2, August 1898

"Only Survivor, The." *Halifax Herald,* October 30 1896.

Paine, Lincoln P. *Down East, A Maritime History of Maine.* Gardner, ME: Tilbury House, 2000.

Port of Saint John. Saint John Port Authority, 2008, www.sjport.com

Quinn, William P. *Shipwrecks Around Maine.* Lower Cape Publishing Company, 1983.

Richardson, John M. *Steamboat Lore of the Penobscot.* Augusta, ME: Kennebec Journal Print Shop, 1941.

Royal Gazette, Saint John, NB. June 29, 1836, Vol., No.1.

Ryan, Allie. *Penobscot Bay Mount Desert and Eastport Steamboat Album.* Camden, ME: Down East Enterprise, Inc. 1972.

Saint John, New Brunswick, Wikipedia, 2008,
Wikipedia.org/wikiSaint_John,_New_Brunswick., June 15,
1934.

Ships and Seafarers of Atlantic Canada. Maritime History Archives,
University of Newfoundland, 1998.

Short, Vincent, and Edwin Sears. *Sail and Steam Along the Maine
Coast.* Portland, ME: The Bond Wheelwright Company,
1955.

Silitch, Clarissa M., ed. *Danger, Disaster and Horrid Deeds,* Dublin,
NH: Yankee, 1974.

Simpson, Dorothy. *The Maine Islands.* Philadelphia, PA: J.B.
Lippincott Company, 1960.

Smith, Barbara, D. *Terror at Sea.* The Provincial Press, Portland,
Maine, 1996.

Snow, Edward R. *Storms and Shipwrecks of New England.* Beverly,
MA: Commonwealth Editions, 2003.

_____. *True Tales of Terrible Shipwrecks.* New York, NY: Dodd, Mead &
Company, 1963.

_____. *Great Storms and Famous Shipwrecks of the New England Coast.*
Boston, MA: Yankee Publishing Company 1943.

"Steamer Royal Tar." *Acadian Recorder,* June 18, 1836.

Stuart, Floyd C. "The Burning of The Circus Ship Royal Tar."
Portland Sunday Telegram, July 20, 1958.

Thayer, Stuart. *Traveling Showmen The American Circus Before the Civil
War.* Detroit, MI: Astley & Ricketts, 1997.

_____. "One Sheet". *Bandwagon.* Vol. 18, No. 5, September-October,
1974.

_____ . *Annals of the American Circus 1793-1860.* Seattle, WA: Dauven
& Thayer, 1976.

"The First Circus Elephants in America". *The White Tops*, December 1940–January 1941.

Thorndike, Virginia L. *How We Got There From Here.* Camden, ME: Down East Books, 1997.

"To The Humane." *Portland Eastern Argus*, November 7, 1836, No. 264, Vol. 2.

U.S. Coast Guard Historian's Office, *Coast Guard History,* 2008, www.uscg.mil/history/

_____. *What is a "Cutter"?* www.uscg.mil/history/FAGS/ Designations.html

Villiers, Alan. *Men, Ships and The Sea.* Washington, DC: National Geographic Society, 1973.

Wallace, Frederick W. *Wooden Ships and Iron Men.* London, U.K.: Hodder and Stoughton, 1924.

Wescott, Allen P. "Loss of the Steamer Royal Tar with a Menagerie Aboard—year 1836*: Bandwagon,* No. 13, July 15, 1944, p.2.

Whittier, Bob. *Paddle Wheel Steamers and Their Giant Engines.* Duxbury, MA: Seamaster, Inc., 1987.

Winslow, Sidney L. *Fish Scales and Stone Chips.* Portland, ME: Machigonne, Press, 1952.

_____. "Intimate Views of Vinalhaven." *Courier Gazette,* December 1, 1944.

Wreck Details. *Northern Shipwrecks Database.* 2008, Northern Maritime Research, Bedford, NS.

Wright, Esther Clark. *Saint John Ships and Their Builders.* Esther Clark Wright, 1976.

Mark Warner is the author of four other
books: *The Best Places to Photograph Wildlife in
North America, On the Button: Practical Advice to
the Nature Photographer, The Appalachian Trail:
An Aerial View,* and *Monhegan: A Guide to
Maine's Fabled Island.* He was raised on the
island of Vinalhaven, and resides in midcoast
Maine.